AIR FRYER COOKBOOK UK XXL

Affordable, Delicious and Super-Amazing Recipes That Will Improve Your Kitchen Game | BONUS: Snacks, Sides & More | Family Favourites for Every Day of the Year

NATHAN ADKINSON

TABLE OF CONTENTS

Desert Delights

Sides & Snacks

EXCLUSIVE BONUS

40 Weight Loss Recipes

&

14 Days Meal Plan

Scan the QR-Code and receive
the FREE download:

Air Fryer Recipe Book

You've probably heard of air frying and are considering purchasing an air fryer yourself. If not, you're probably one of many people that have already invested in one and have found it to be a great way to cook. Of course, any new technology can be daunting.

The good news is air fryers are exceptionally easy to use and you're in the right place to find out everything you need to know. If you're already an expert on the machine then you can head straight to the impressive and delicious selection of recipes, including suggestions for breakfast, lunch, dinner, desserts, and even snacks. There is certain to be something that titillates your tastebuds.

Introducing The Air Fryer

The air fryer was first invented as long ago as 1946! It was created by William L. Maxson, a man who had gradually become obsessed with the possibility of reheating food and maintaining flavours. His realization that air, suitably heated, could pass around food and cook it or reheat it, led to his first patent, something that today would be called an electric oven.

The following year saw him create a rudimentary air fryer. It was a heavy machine but used by the military and later commercial airlines. Unfortunately, he died before the air fryer became mainstream. The invention of the microwave appeared to leave the air fryer as a distant memory.

But, technology was still developing and in 2010 Phillips launched their own air fryer. This one was small and light enough to be used by people at home. Since then, publicity and awareness of the air fryer have made it an increasingly popular item to have in the home.

How The Air Fryer Works

The air fryer is a cross between a conventional oven and an oil fryer. Its design is similar to an oil fryer, generally oval in shape with a basket where food is placed. This is important as it allows heated air to be moved around inside the air fryer. A motor is included in the design to generate and move this hot air. This is effectively a fan located near the heating element. The element warms the air and the fan pushes it around the chamber

The main difference between the air fryer and the oven is that an oven pushes heat in one direction, while the air fryer moves it all around the chamber.

Air fryers have a variety of settings, this includes cooking, broiling, searing, and even dehydrating. That makes them an exceptionally useful tool.

Why It Is A Good Choice

Modern air fryers are small, they are energy efficient, and also powerful. In short, they are capable of reaching the same temperatures as your oven. Their size and weight mean you can easily move them around your kitchen or even take it to a friend's house.

It's worth noting that the air fryer comes in two distinct styles.

Basket

The basket style air fryer is similar inside to a deep fat fryer, without the oil. A basket holds the food and this is lowered into the heated fryer. Air can move freely around the food, cooking it without deep frying it. The basket can then be lifted out to remove the food and serve.

Oven

The oven style air fryer doesn't use a basket, it is more like a conventional oven. You simply place your food on the included baking tray and slide it into the air fryer. The air can move effortlessly around it and cook the food in the same way and time as a basket fryer.

It should be noted that many of the recipes in this book mention putting food into the air fryer basket. The recipes work just as well with an oven style air fryer. Simply place the food on the tray instead of in the basket.

How To Use An Air Fryer

Air fryers can appear a little daunting for the first-time user. The same can be said of any new technology. However, the good news is they are very simple to use. The first thing you need to do is familiarize yourself with your chosen air fryer.

That means assessing whether it is a basket or oven style, what functions it has, and how high a temperature it can reach. The majority of air fryers have LCD panels on the front or somewhere easily visible. This is where you can set the temperature or choose the cooking mode.

On higher-level models, this panel will also have additional features, such as a timer or pre-programmed settings to cover certain food items.

Once you have become familiar with how your air fryer works, you'll be able to start using it. But, before you place anything into the fryer you'll want to stop things from sticking to the basket or the baking tray. Most people spray the basket or tray with cooking spray as this prevents food from sticking. However, if you prefer you can use parchment paper, also known as greaseproof paper.

Your air fryer does need a small amount of oil in the bottom drawer. In most cases, this needs to be oil not cooking spray. You'll need to check your instruction manual for the exact amount of oil to add.

Once you've prepared your air fryer you can turn it on and select the desired temperature. Once it has reached temperature simply add your food to the basket or tray and close the lid. It is important to spread food evenly around the basket. This allows maximum airflow across the food and ensures even cooking.

Your machine will probably have a timer built in. That will ensure you leave the food in for just the right amount of time.

There are several advantages and disadvantages of an air fryer:

Pros

Less oil

Perhaps the most obvious advantage is the reduced use of oil. Air fryers need a tiny amount of oil in the bottom of them and you may spray some food items with oil prior to cooking. The oil helps the air to circulate efficiently and it helps to ensure your food crisps properly. This effectively eliminates the pale colour so often given when food is microwaved.

Considering the ever-increasing price of oil this can represent a significant cost saving.

Less mess

There is no escaping the fact that oil is messy. It doesn't matter what you do when using a deep fat fryer, you will end up with oil on the work surfaces and your hands. This makes a mess, increases cleaning up time, and the oil can even cause issues in your drainage system.

That mess is avoided with an air fryer.

Healthier

Deep fat frying gives food a distinctive and often desirable taste. However, all that oil is not good for your body. It helps to increase body fat levels and clog arteries, effectively boosting the likelihood of you contracting an array of age-related diseases.

The air fryer uses a very small amount of oil, effectively cooking in the air. That makes it a significantly healthier option and a desirable addition to every kitchen.

Reduced fire risk

It's estimated that deep fat fryers cause one fifth of all house fires in the UK. In fact, approximately 20 people are killed or injured daily thanks to a home fire that started in the kitchen.

The biggest issue when a deep fat fryer becomes ablaze is that the intense blaze is not easy to put out. This isn't an issue if you have an air fryer. There isn't enough oil in it to cause a fire, making it a far safer and healthier option than your deep fat fryer.

Cons

Naturally, there are some drawbacks to the air fryer:

They are small

Air fryers come in a range of sizes, from very small ones designed for one person to family-sized ones. But, regardless of which size you choose, there are some food items that can't be fitted inside your air fryer.

Size also means that you'll often have to cook food in batches, staggering eating times. That's something most people don't like.

They Are Slower

Air fryers can reach high temperatures. But, as it is air being heated, the air fryer can't compete with the temperature extremes offered by deep fat fryers. That means things in air fryers tend to take longer to cook.

Of course, this is offset by its many advantages but it is worth noting.

Not all foods can be cooked in them

Air fryers are useful and can cook a wide variety of foods; However, there are some food items that simply can't be put into the air fryer.

Crowding

It's very important that food isn't crowded when you're using an air fryer. Crowding is when food is touching each other. This reduces the amount of air that can flow around the food and effectively lowers the temperature the food is exposed to. In other words, if the food is too crowded it won't be properly cooked.

Maintenance Tips

The first part of maintenance is cleaning. It's important to keep your machine clean as this will ensure it works efficiently and effectively.

Basic Cleaning

Basic cleaning should be carried out every time you use your air fryer. This will ensure the elements are clean and ready to work efficiently and effectively. Here's what you need to do:
- Unplug your air fryer first to prevent accidentally turning it on or electrocuting yourself

- ❧ Take the air fryer basket out of the machine and slide the bottom drawer out of place
- ❧ The basket and drawer can be washed in warm soapy water. But, remember to dispose of any remaining oil properly
- ❧ You can use baking soda to remove any stubborn stains on the basket, tray, or bottom drawer. If you do this every time there shouldn't be any stubborn stains
- ❧ Give the outside of your machine a wipe over with a clean damp cloth
- ❧ Dry everything properly before putting it back together

It's worth noting that some air fryer baskets and trays can be put in the dishwasher, making this process even simpler. You'll need to check in your manual whether your machine is dishwasher safe or not.

A Deep Clean

Periodically you should undertake a deep clean. This will help to ensure your machine is working properly. A deep clean can be done every couple of months, but only if you use the machine regularly

The deep clean involves scrubbing the inside of the machine as well. Again, baking soda mixed with water creates a paste that can remove most stains. In other instances, warm soapy water will suffice. Just make sure the machine is dried properly before you start using it again.

In addition, you should note the following:

Less is more when it comes to oil

An air fryer can be used without oil, especially if there is oil in the food you're cooking. However, it works more efficiently if it has a little oil in it. But, the critical factor is a small amount. It's easy to put more oil than you need in the fryer.

Check your handbook before you start using it and add the right amount of oil.

Preheat first

Before you start cooking in your air fryer make sure you give it time to warm up. That means, turning it on when you start preparing food and making sure it has reached the right temperature before you put the food in the air fryer.

If you don't, the food won't be cooked at the proper temperature and is likely to be undercooked. This can result in health issues. In addition, you may be tempted to cook the items for longer which can cause them to dry out.

Check if dishwasher safe

As mentioned in the cleaning guidelines, you should always check whether the air fryer items can be put in a dishwasher or not. Obviously, the main fryer can't be as it is electrical. But the basket and tray often can be.

However, if they are not dishwasher safe or you don't know then don't risk it, you're likely to damage the non-stick coating and prevent the machine from working properly.

Know your own machine

The bottom line is simple, you need to know everything about your machine in order to use it effectively and keep it in the best possible condition. The easiest way to do this is to read the guide that comes with your machine and make sure you understand it before you turn it on for the first time.

Part of reading the guide ensures you know the temperatures your machine can reach and how long it takes to get to the right temperature. That is important when considering preparation time. It allows you to create a balance between energy usage and minimizing cooking preparation time.

Additional Facts You Should Know

There are several other things you should know about your air fryer:

Foods to avoid cooking in an air fryer

Air fryers are a fantastic way of cooking many items. However, just like any machine, they have their limitations. This includes foods that can't be cooked in the air fryer.

For example:

Foods with wet batter

Any food that has a wet batter is likely to drip inside your machine while it's being cooked. The result is a mess that can be hard to clean off and the food won't taste as you expect.

Broccoli

Most vegetables cook okay in the air fryer but broccoli doesn't. The air fryer will suck the moisture out of the broccoli, leaving it hard or potentially as dust.

Whole roast

Your air fryer is unlikely to be large enough to handle an entire roast or even a large chicken. Alongside this, the air fryer may struggle to cook the inside of the meat thoroughly, leaving you with a crispy outside and an uncooked centre. That's never a good plan.

Rice

Rice and any other dried foods need to be rehydrated. As an air fryer sucks moisture from foods, it is never going to rehydrate your rice and cook it properly.

While there are inserts that will allow you to add water and soak your rice while cooking it in the air fryer, this is not an effective mechanism. The air fryer won't heat the water hot enough to get the desired result.

Foods with dry seasonings

The air fryer uses a fan to circulate heat, ensuring it is evenly distributed across all of the food. However, this does mean that any dry seasoning is likely to be blown off the food. You will have unseasoned food and a mess in the bottom of your air fryer.

Don't overfill it

Air fryers rely on air circulating around the food. This heats the food and ensures it is cooked properly. If the air can't circulate properly then the food won't be evenly cooked.

In short, layer the basket or have food touching each other and you're unlikely to get food that is cooked properly.

In short, don't overfill the machine.

Give it a shake

If you have laid your food in the fryer properly then it should cook evenly. However, there is no harm in lifting the basket out halfway through the cooking process and giving the food a shake. Ideally, you should turn all the food items over to ensure they are cooked evenly and go a nice shade of golden brown.

Put water in the bottom tray

Air fryers use a tiny amount of oil. However, the heat inside the fryer will cause the oil to evaporate and you'll end up with smoke. That's never desirable.

Fortunately, you can eliminate this issue by adding a spoon or two of water to the bottom of your machine. It heats and mingles with the oil, preventing smoking while still allowing your food to crisp up perfectly.

Line your basket

One of the biggest issues with an air fryer is the time it takes to clean it after use. However, it doesn't need to be time-consuming. Line your basket or tray with parchment paper. This will absorb any grease, preventing it from dripping onto the bottom of the air fryer and causing an array of issues.

It is okay to use standard parchment paper. However, you may prefer to use some designed for your air fryer. It has small holes that help the air to circulate while the paper still captures the oil and other mess dripping from your food.

It can be a process of trial and error to get perfect results from your air fryer. However, this process is worth it as an air fryer is a useful addition to any kitchen. Once you've mastered your machine, you'll be able to dazzle family and friends with the following recipes.

EXCLUSIVE BONUS

40 Weight Loss Recipes

&

14 Days Meal Plan

Scan the QR-Code and receive
the FREE download:

Recipes

BREAKFAST OPTIONS

Vegetable Omelette

SERVES 1
PREP TIME: 5 MINUTES | TOTAL: 15 MINUTES
NET CARBS: 10G | PROTEIN: 18.2G | FIBRE: 4.9G | FAT: 28G
KCAL: 398

INGREDIENTS

- 2 eggs
- 125ml milk
- sliced peppers, onions, mushrooms – as many or as few as you want
- 125g grated cheese
- Pinch of salt - optional

INSTRUCTIONS

1. Break the eggs into a bowl and add the milk, then beat them well
2. Throw in your vegetables and salt (if using) and mix
3. Pour the mixture into a standard pan, make sure this will fit inside the basket of your air fryer
4. Preheat the air fryer to 180°C
5. Put the basket with pan into the fryer and cook for 10 minutes
6. Lift the basket out and cover the omelette with the cheese
7. Lift it out and garnish before serving/eating

Breakfast Sausage

PER SAUSAGE
PREP TIME: 15 MINUTES | TOTAL: 15 MINUTES
NET CARBS: 3G | PROTEIN: 14G | FIBRE: 3.9G | FAT: 21G
KCAL: 260

INGREDIENTS

- Sausages – as many as you like and any flavour you like!
- Peppers

- Parchment paper – not to be eaten

INSTRUCTIONS

1. Preheat your air fryer to 200°C
2. Start by lining the basket of your air fryer with parchment paper. It will soak up grease from the sausage. If you don't your air fryer will smoke
3. Put as many sausages as you want or can fit into the basket. It doesn't matter if they touch each other but there should only be one layer of sausages
4. Cook the sausages for 15 minutes
5. Open the air fryer and turn the sausages over, then cook for another 5 minutes
6. Serve with diced pepper, bread, or anything else you fancy
7. Don't forget they will be very hot

Bacon & Egg Bites

PER EGG BITE
PREP TIME: 15 MINUTES | TOTAL: 25 MINUTES
NET CARBS: 2G | PROTEIN: 8G | FIBRE: 3G | FAT: 9G
KCAL: 119

INGREDIENTS

- 6 eggs
- 2 tablespoons milk
- 1 chopped green pepper
- 1 chopped red pepper
- A sliced and diced onion
- A handful of fresh spinach - chopped
- 125g of cheddar cheese
- 50g mozzarella cheese
- 3 slices cooked bacon - crumbled
- Small silicone moulds

INSTRUCTIONS

1. Preheat the air fryer to 160°C – these are best when cooked slower
2. Put your eggs in a mixing bowl and add your milk and salt/pepper if desired. Whisk thoroughly until blended
3. Add your peppers, onions, and spinach and combine carefully
4. Then add your cheese and bacon, make sure you blend it slowly while whisking continuously
5. Place the silicone moulds in your air fryer basket. You should be able to fill six of them
6. Pour the mixture into the moulds and carefully lower the basket into the fryer
7. Add an extra sprinkling of cheese, if desired
8. Cook for 15 minutes, a toothpick can be used to check they are cooked. It should be put in the centre and emerge clean
9. Enjoy with garnish or by themselves

Loaded Hash Browns

SERVES 4
PREP TIME: 30 MINUTES | TOTAL: 45-50 MINUTES
NET CARBS: 12.7G | PROTEIN: 6.1G | FIBRE: 4.3G | FAT: 21G
KCAL: 264

INGREDIENTS

- 6 good-sized sweet potatoes
- 1 tsp paprika
- 1 garlic clove crushed
- 1 1 tablespoon olive oil
- 1 green pepper chopped and one red pepper chopped
- 1 onion finely sliced
- 100g grated cheese

INSTRUCTIONS

1. Start by grating your potatoes. You'll want to use the largest size on your grater
2. Now soak the potatoes for 25 minutes
3. Drain the liquid from the potatoes and put them in a dry bowl
4. Tadd the paprika, olive oil, and garlic. You can use salt and pepper but this is optional
5. Toss the potatoes to ensure they are fully coated in the mix
6. Put them in the air fryer basket and preheat the air fryer to 220°C
7. Cook them for approximately 18 minutes until crispy
8. Remove and place on your plate, then sprinkle green and red peppers with onion and grated cheese across the top of them

Egg Tarts

SERVES 4
PREP TIME: 5 MINUTES | TOTAL: 25 MINUTES
NET CARBS: 12.5G | PROTEIN: 17.4G | FIBRE: 4.7G | FAT: 27G
KCAL: 345

INGREDIENTS

- 1 sheet puff pastry – if you're using frozen make sure it is thawed before you start
- 200g grated cheese – your choice of cheese
- 4 eggs
- Large pinch of freshly chopped parsley
- Spoonful of flour

INSTRUCTIONS

1. Start by preheating your air fryer to 200°C
2. While the air fryer is heating lay out your pastry sheet flat.
3. Cut the pastry sheet into four equal pieces
4. Put the pieces in your air fryer basket, then air fry for 10 minutes. Depending on the size of your basket you may need to do this in two sessions
5. As soon as you open the air fryer use a metal spoon to create an indent in each piece of pastry. Simply press down hard on it
6. Sprinkle a quarter of your cheese into each indent
7. Crack an egg into each indent on top of the cheese
8. Put back in the air fryer for another 10 minutes
9. Remove and transfer to a wire rack to cool for several minutes before serving

Breakfast Taquito

SERVES 2
PREP TIME: 5 MINUTES | TOTAL: 13 MINUTES
NET CARBS: 20G | PROTEIN: 17G | FIBRE: 1G | FAT: 22G
KCAL: 352

INGREDIENTS

- 1 flatbread wrap
- 2 eggs – you'll need to scramble these in the conventional way
- 2 slices bacon cooked and crumbled
- 50g grated cheese – ideally cheddar but it can be anything you like
- 1 tablespoon fresh pico, (a mix of tomatoes, onions, and peppers)

INSTRUCTIONS

1. Step one is to get the air fryer heated up. It should be set to 180°C
2. Next, lay the bread wrap out flat
3. Add the scrambled eggs and the bacon to the bread wrap. Place these items on one side only
4. Sprinkle the grated cheese across the top of the egg and bacon
5. Add your fresh pico and any other herbs you think would enhance the flavour
6. Roll the flatbread up then cut it in half
7. Place it in the air fryer basket and cook for 8 minutes
8. Remove carefully from the air fryer, the taquitos will be hot
9. Serve with some salsa if desired

Biscuit Bombs

SERVES 10
PREP TIME: 30 MINUTES | TOTAL: 45 MINUTES
NET CARBS: 13G | PROTEIN: 7G | FIBRE: 5.2G | FAT: 13G
KCAL: 190

INGREDIENTS

- 400g sausage
- 2 eggs – give them a good beating
- 1 sheet pastry
- 125g cheese cut into small squares
- Salt and pepper if desired
- 1 tablespoon olive oil
- Additional egg
- Tablespoon of water

INSTRUCTIONS

1. The first thing to do is preheat the air fryer to 150°C
2. Put a circle of parchment paper at the bottom of your air basket
3. Cook your sausages in a conventional frying pan with a little oil for approximately 5 minutes
4. When the sausages are cooked remove them and place them in a small bowl
5. Add the eggs and any salt and pepper to the frying pan and cook until they start to thicken
6. Allow the eggs to cool for several minutes
7. Separate the pastry into ten pieces and create indents in the middle
8. Add your eggs and sausage to the centre of each piece of pastry
9. Wrap the pastry around the ingredients and push the pastry together at the top
10. Add a piece of cheese to the top of the pastry
11. Mix the egg and tablespoon of water in a separate bowl
12. Brush the egg mix onto the pastry on all sides.
13. Now place them in your air basket, you can layer them with a sheet of parchment between them, and cook for 8 minutes
14. Enjoy when cooled slightly

Breakfast Burritos

SERVES 2
PREP TIME: 10 MINUTES | TOTAL: 15 MINUTES
NET CARBS: 15G | PROTEIN: 21G | FIBRE: 8G | FAT: 27G
KCAL: 358

INGREDIENTS

- 2 flour tortillas
- 2 eggs – scramble them before you start the recipe
- 3 slices of bacon – grilled then crumbled
- 1 pepper – your choice of colour
- 1 150g grated cheese – cheddar is normally used but any type of cheese will do
- 4 sausages – cook them and then crumble them when cooled
- A little olive oil in a spray bottle – if required

INSTRUCTIONS

1. Preheat the air fryer to 150°C
2. Start by placing the scrambled eggs in a bowl with your cooked and crumbled sausage
3. Add the peppers and small pieces of bacon along with the cheese and mix it together thoroughly
4. Lay out one flour tortilla
5. Add approximately half the mixture to the middle of the tortilla
6. Lift the sides and roll the tortilla to create your burrito
7. Repeat the process with a second tortilla to make another burrito
8. Cook in your air fryer for 5 minutes
9. Allow to cool for a few minutes before eating

French Toast

MAKES 12
PREP TIME: 7 MINUTES | TOTAL: 15 MINUTES
NET CARBS: 12G | PROTEIN: 6G | FIBRE: 1G | FAT: 8G
KCAL: 170

A simple and delicious option that you have the time to make when using an air fryer! It's worth noting you can make more and freeze them for next time.

INGREDIENTS

- 12 slices of bread – white is best but you can use your favourite
- 5 eggs
- 250ml milk
- 250g butter – you'll want to melt this first
- 1 teaspoon vanilla extract
- 1 125g sugar
- 1 tablespoon cinnamon

INSTRUCTIONS

1. Preheat your air fryer to 175˚C
2. Now cut each slice of bread into three pieces, they should all be roughly the same size
3. Grab a medium-sized bowl and break the eggs into it. Add your melted butter and the teaspoon of vanilla – whisk these ingredients until fully blended
4. Mix the cinnamon and sugar together in a separate bowl
5. Dip a piece of bread into the egg mixture, making sure it is covered
6. Now sprinkle the cinnamon mix over both sides of the bread
7. Put each strip in your air fryer and, when the basket is full, cook them for 8 minutes
8. Repeat, if necessary, with the other pieces of bread
9. Allow to cool for a few moments before enjoying

Bacon & Egg Cups

SERVES 4
PREP TIME: 5 MINUTES | TOTAL: 15 MINUTES
NET CARBS: 12G | PROTEIN: 18G | FIBRE: 7G | FAT: 12G
KCAL: 198

INGREDIENTS

- 1 packet thin cut fat-free bacon
- 4 eggs – the larger the better
- 1 onion, peeled and then finely sliced
- Some salt and pepper as desired to enhance the flavour

INSTRUCTIONS

1. Preheat your air fryer to 180°C
2. Cut the bacon slices into thirds and place them into your air fryer basket, be careful not to let them overlap
3. Cook them for 5 minutes
4. Put four cake wrappers or silicone moulds on the side
5. Add three pieces of partially cooked bacon to each case
6. Break open one of the eggs and empty it into the wrapper, the bacon will provide support. Repeat this for the other three cases
7. Add the finely sliced onion and some salt and pepper as desired, you can also add pieces of pepper if you wish
8. Turn the air fryer up to 200°C and place the four cases carefully in the fryer
9. Cook for 8-12 minutes depending on how soft or hard you like your eggs
10. Remove them from the air fryer and serve them immediately

Air Fried Bagel

SERVES 4
PREP TIME: 5 MINUTES | TOTAL: 15 MINUTES
NET CARBS: 26G | PROTEIN: 10G | FIBRE: 2G | FAT: 1G
KCAL: 152

INGREDIENTS

- 250 g flour – you can choose plain, whole wheat or even a gluten-free flour
- 2 tsp baking powder
- 1 large egg – you'll need to break this into a cup and beat it first
- An individual Greek yoghurt
- Pinch of salt and pepper if desired
- Toppings of your choice, such as sesame seeds

1. Preheat your air fryer to 210°C
2. Mix together your flour with the baking powder and any salt or pepper you desire. A light mix will do
3. Slowly add your Greek yoghurt while stirring to ensure it is fully integrated
4. The mixture should appear crumbly
5. Put a little flour on the side then tip your bagel dough onto the flour
6. Knead the dough to ensure it is a little sticky but not sticky enough to stick to your hand
7. Form four balls from the dough
8. Each ball should be rolled out, allowing you to turn it into a circle with a hole in the middle
9. Roll the dough in your chosen topping then place it in the air fryer basket
10. Cook for 15 minutes, it should look a golden yellow colour
11. Allow them to cool for 10 minutes before enjoying

Breakfast Taquito

SERVES 2
PREP TIME: 5 MINUTES | TOTAL: 15 MINUTES
NET CARBS: 20G | PROTEIN: 17G | FIBRE: 1G | FAT: 22G
KCAL: 352

INGREDIENTS

- 2 large wraps – whole wheat or plain, your choice
- 2 large eggs – you'll need to scramble these before they can go in the air fryer
- 2 slices of bacon – grill them for 5-10 minutes until crispy
- 50g grated cheddar – you can use another cheese if you prefer

INSTRUCTIONS

1. Turn the air fryer on and set it to 190°C
2. Lay one of the wraps out flat and put half the scrambled egg on it along with one slice of bacon. Crumble the bacon as you put it on the wrap
3. Sprinkle half your grated cheese across the top and roll the wrap up
4. Repeat the process with the second wrap
5. Place both wraps in the air fryer basket, you can use a cocktail stick to keep the wraps closed
6. Spray them lightly with cooking oil
7. Put the basket in the preheated air fryer and cook for eight minutes
8. Enjoy by themselves or with a dressing of your choice

Sweet Potato Mix

SERVES 6
PREP TIME: 10 MINUTES | TOTAL: 25 MINUTES
NET CARBS: 31G | PROTEIN: 4G | FIBRE: 3G | FAT: 6G
KCAL: 191

INGREDIENTS

- 2 tbsp olive oil
- 3 sweet potatoes, you don't need to peel them simply cut them into small chunks
- 3 slices bacon – you'll need to cut this into bite-sized pieces. It's best to choose lean bacon
- 1 tsp paprika
- 1 tsp dried dill
- Pinch of salt and pepper to taste

INSTRUCTIONS

1. The first step is to turn, the air fryer on and set the temperature to 200°C
2. Put your small pieces of bacon with your chunks of sweet potato in a bowl. Add the olive oil, paprika, dill, and any salt and pepper you desire
3. Once fully blended together place the mixture onto some greaseproof paper in your air fryer basket
4. Lower the basket into the fryer and cook for 15 minutes
5. You'll want to check and toss it every 3-4 minutes
6. Once its browned remove it from the air fryer and serve straight away with some warm fresh bread

Fantastic Frittata

SERVES 2
PREP TIME: 15 MINUTES | TOTAL: 35 MINUTES
NET CARBS: 3G | PROTEIN: 31G | FIBRE: 5G | FAT: 27G
KCAL: 380

INGREDIENTS

- 2 tbsp olive oil
- 4 sausages – you can choose your preferred flavour and type. They'll need to be cooked under the grill until brown, then, let them cool a little before crumbling them
- 4 eggs – put them in a bowl and beat them, preferably without the shells
- 1100g cheddar grated, you can use any cheese
- 1 red pepper – deseeded and cut into slices
- 1 onion – peeled and finely sliced
- Pinch of salt and pepper – if desired

1. Turn the air fryer on and set the temperature to 180°C
2. Run a little of the olive oil around a non-stick pan, approximately 15cm in diameter. This is to stop the frittata from sticking
3. Mix your crumbled sausage into the beaten eggs then add the pepper, onion, and cheese. You can also add a little salt and pepper if you wish
4. After you've thoroughly mixed the ingredients tip them into your non-stick oven pan
5. Drop the pan into the air fryer basket or onto the baking tray and cook for 20 minutes
6. Remove and enjoy straight away

Flat Sausage

SERVES 4
PREP TIME: 5 MINUTES | TOTAL: 15 MINUTES
NET CARBS: 8G | PROTEIN: 14G | FIBRE: 4G | FAT: 9G
KCAL: 145

INGREDIENTS

- 500g sausages – choose your preferred flavour
- Cooking oil spray
- Salt and pepper to taste
- 1 peeled and chopped onion

INSTRUCTIONS

1. Start by heating your air fryer to 200°C
2. Next, break the sausages up into pieces, much the same as ground beef. You can choose to use sausage meat if you prefer
3. Put the crumbled sausage in a bowl with the onion and combine
4. Divide the sausage meat into four equal portions
5. Take one portion and squeeze it in your hands until you make a burger-shape
6. Repeat with the other three portions
7. Line your air fryer basket with a piece of greaseproof and drop the sausage patties into the basket
8. Cook in the air fryer for approximately 8 minutes, and flip the patties halfway through the cooking process. The middle of the pattie should be at least 70°C
9. Remove them and serve straight away, you can eat them by themselves or add any dressing or side dish you wish

Toad In The Hole

SERVES 4
PREP TIME: 5 MINUTES | TOTAL: 30 MINUTES
NET CARBS: 28G | PROTEIN: 14G | FIBRE: 8G | FAT: 31G
KCAL: 446

INGREDIENTS

- 1 packet of shop-bought puff pastry, you only need one sheet out of the packet and you can make your own puff pastry if you prefer
- 75g cheddar cheese
- 75g ham – it needs to be cooked and sliced into small pieces, or you can buy it this way
- 1 tbsp chives
- 4 large eggs

1. Preheat your air fryer to 200°C
2. Either make your puff pastry and lay it on the side or open the packet and lay one sheet of the shop-bought pastry on your side
3. Cut the pastry into four equal-sized pieces
4. Put two of the squares in the bottom of your air fryer basket and cook them for 6 minutes
5. Remove the squares and using the back of a spoon, press down on them while still warm. You'll cause an indentation
6. Scoop a quarter of the cheese into the indentation and half the ham. Push it down and then add the egg
7. Repeat for the second pastry square and then put them both in your air fryer for another 6 minutes.
8. Remove them and repeat the process for the other two. If your air fryer is big enough you can do all four at the same time
9. Once cooked serve immediately

Breakfast Pockets

SERVES 8
PREP TIME: 10 MINUTES | TOTAL: 20 MINUTES
NET CARBS: 23G | PROTEIN: 14G | FIBRE: 9G | FAT: 23G
KCAL: 363

INGREDIENTS

- 10 croissants, you can use fresh or refrigerated ones
- 10 sausages – choose your preferred flavour
- 50g butter
- 4 eggs – the larger the better
- 100g cheese grated; cheddar is best but any type can be used
- Salt and pepper as desired

INSTRUCTIONS

1. As usual, put your air fryer in a good position and turn it to 175°C, allow it to heat up before putting anything in it
2. Take each croissant and cut it down the middle, it's best to make the cut across the top as this minimizes mess in the air fryer
3. In a pan over a medium heat put your butter and sausages
4. As the butter melts make sure the sausages are coated, they should go a golden brown in 5-10 minutes
5. Add your eggs and any salt and pepper you wish, and cook for another 2-3 minutes
6. Put an equal amount of the filling in each of your croissants and sprinkle your cheese across the top
7. Lower as many as you can into the air fryer, making sure they don't touch each other
8. Cook for 5 minutes, they will go golden and you can repeat this for the other croissants
9. Serve and enjoy straight away

LUNCH CHOICES

Meatballs In Tomato Sauce

SERVES 3-4
PREP TIME: 15 MINUTES | TOTAL: 30 MINUTES
NET CARBS: 10G | PROTEIN: 8G | FIBRE: 2G | FAT: 21G
KCAL: 270

INGREDIENTS

- 20 meatballs – you can buy them ready-made or make them yourself
- Jar of your favourite pasta sauce
- 24 mushrooms finely chopped
- 1 onion sliced
- 1 tsp oil
- 1 clove garlic - chopped
- 1 sprig of fresh parsley

INSTRUCTIONS

1. The first step is to heat your air fryer to 180°C
2. Once it has reached temperature, place your meatballs into the basket and lower it into the fryer. It's best to leave a small space around each meatball
3. Cook for roughly 12 minutes, until the meatballs look golden
4. Separately? Ina standard frying pan, put your tsp of oil and heat it up
5. Add the onion and garlic and simmer gently
6. When they go translucent add your mushrooms
7. After a few minutes add your jar of pasta sauce – keep stirring while you do this
8. As soon as your meatballs are cooked, add them to the sauce and allow to simmer for a couple of minutes
9. Now serve and enjoy

You can have them by themselves, with some fresh bread, mashed potato, or even in a long bun.

French Toasted Cheese Sandwich

PER SANDWICH
PREP TIME: 15 MINUTES | TOTAL: 15 MINUTES
NET CARBS: 39G | PROTEIN: 41G | FIBRE: 10G | FAT: 25G
KCAL: 650

INGREDIENTS

- 1 box pancake mix – if you prefer you can make the pancake batter yourself
- 1 large egg
- 250ml milk
- 125ml water
- 1 teaspoon vanilla essence or extract
- 8 slices Swiss cheese
- 8 slices ham
- 8 slices toast

INSTRUCTIONS

1. Start by preheating your air fryer to 175°C
2. Mix your milk, water, vanilla essence, and the box of pancake mix in a bowl. Make sure the ingredients are well blended
3. You want the mixture to be thick, add the pancake mix slowly as this thickens it
4. Make your sandwich – that's a slice of bread, a piece of cheese, two pieces of ham, and another piece of cheese. Finish with a second slice of bread
5. Use a toothpick to hold the corners of the sandwich together
6. Place the sandwich in your thick batter mix, making sure both sides are coated
7. Now place it in the air fryer basket and into the air fryer
8. Cook for ten minutes, flipping halfway through
9. Enjoy it by itself, with garnish, or with some potato chips

Hot Turkey Sandwich

PER SANDWICH
PREP TIME: 15 MINUTES | TOTAL: 15 MINUTES
NET CARBS: 29G | PROTEIN: 18G | FIBRE: 7G | FAT: 20G
KCAL: 450

Why go to the deli when you can make this delicious turkey sandwich at home!

INGREDIENTS

- 2 slices of bread – white works best but any will do
- 3 slices turkey
- 2 slices of your favourite cheese
- 25g butter
- Pinch of freshly chopped parsley
- Garlic clove crushed or a teaspoon of garlic powder
- 1 little olive oil in a spray bottle

INSTRUCTIONS

1. Your air fryer will need to be 200°C, it's best to put it on first to warm up
2. Lay the bread on the side and spread each slice with butter
3. Add the garlic and the parsley to one slice of bread. Note, these ingredients are optional, if you don't like them substitute them or leave them out
4. Place one slice of cheese on a piece of bread, then the 3 turkey slices, followed by the other slice of cheese and the second piece of bread on top. Your sandwich is made
5. Lightly spray one side of the sandwich with oil
6. Line the air fryer basket with parchment paper and lay the oil side of the sandwich on it
7. Spray the other side of the sandwich and lower it into the air fryer
8. Cook for 5 minutes and then you're ready to serve

French Bread Pizza

SERVES 4
PREP TIME: 15 MINUTES | TOTAL: 15 MINUTES
NET CARBS: 243G | PROTEIN: 17G | FIBRE: 3G | FAT: 12G
KCAL: 344

INGREDIENTS

- 1 French baguette
- 1 small tin tomato paste
- 2100g grated cheese
- ½ green pepper chopped
- ½ onion chopped
- Several pieces of chorizo
- Salt and pepper if desired

INSTRUCTIONS

1. As always, start by turning the air fryer on and setting it to 200°C, this will give it chance to warm up
2. Cut your French baguette into three or four pieces, they need to be small enough to fit in your air fryer
3. Cover each pierce with the tomato paste
4. Add a layer of chorizo slices to each piece of French bread
5. Sprinkle onions and pepper across the baguette
6. Follow this with a heavy coat of cheese
7. Drop the baguette into the air fryer basket and cook for 5 minutes. You can cook for longer if you wish but remember that it cooks quickly, check it every minute
8. You may need tongs to remove it
9. Repeat for additional pieces of baguette

Beef Gyros

SERVES 3
PREP TIME: 10 MINUTES | TOTAL: 25 MINUTES
NET CARBS: 58G | PROTEIN: 46G | FIBRE: 4G | FAT: 9G
KCAL: 587

When you're in a rush this is a great choice, it's easy, fast, and delicious!

INGREDIENTS

- 500g beef – shave it into thin slices
- 1 onion chopped
- 3 pitta breads – your choice of whole wheat or regular
- 1 lettuce, pickles, cucumber, and other garnishes – these are not obligatory
- 1 tablespoon of olive oil
- 2 tablespoons of Greek seasoning – you should find it in your local supermarket
- 1 Greek yoghurt
- 2 cloves garlic crushed
- Pinch of dill, parsley, or basil
- Pinch of salt and pepper – again, not obligatory

INSTRUCTIONS

1. Preheat your air fryer to 180°C

2. Mix together your thinly sliced or shaved beef with the oil and your Greek seasoning. Make sure it is all fully coated

3. Line the air fryer basket with parchment or silver foil to keep all the juices in the right place

4. Place the beef mixture in the air fryer basket and cook for 8-10 minutes. This can be adjusted depending on how you prefer your beef

5. While it's cooking you can peel a cucumber and then cut it into long slices, and dice these to make cubes. You can then blend them until they are pureed

6. Now place the cucumber, Greek yoghurt, herbs, garlic, and onion in a bowl and mix them together. Add salt if you wish

7. Open your pitta bread and fill it with the sauce and your beef mixture. Repeat with the other two pittas and enjoy the explosion of flavours in your mouth

Catfish Pretzel

SERVES 4
PREP TIME: 15 MINUTES | TOTAL: 25 MINUTES
NET CARBS: 45G | PROTEIN: 33G | FIBRE: 2G | FAT: 14G
KCAL: 466

INGREDIENTS

- 4 catfish fillets
- 2 eggs
- 250g flour
- 2 tablespoons milk
- 1 large bag honey coated pretzels – you'll need to crush these, it's easiest to do while they are in the bag
- 2 tablespoons Dijon mustard
- Pinch salt and pepper – to desired taste
- Olive oil in a spray bottle

INSTRUCTIONS

1. Your air fryer will need to be preheated to 175°C
2. Start by laying your catfish fillets on a suitable surface and sprinkle them with the desired amount of salt and pepper
3. Separately, put your eggs in a bowl and beat them
4. Add your mustard and the milk and whisk with the eggs
5. Put your flour in another bowl and the crushed pretzels in a further bowl
6. Line your air fryer basket with parchment
7. Take each catfish fillet and dip it into the flour, ensuring it's fully coated. Then dip it into the milk mix and, again, ensure its fully coated
8. Finally, roll it in the pretzel crumbs and place it in the air fryer basket
9. When all the fillets are in the basket, (assuming they fit in one go), put them in the air fryer for 10 minutes
10. Remove and enjoy with a light salad for lunch

Chicken Tenderloin

SERVES 4
PREP TIME: 15 MINUTES | TOTAL: 27 MINUTES
NET CARBS: 10G | PROTEIN: 26G | FIBRE: 2G | FAT: 11G
KCAL: 253

INGREDIENTS

- 1 egg
- 8 chicken tenderloins or sliced chicken breasts – your choice
- 2 tablespoons vegetable oil
- 250g bread crumbs
- 8 carrots
- 1 cucumber
- 4 sticks of celery

INSTRUCTIONS

1. Start by preheating your air fryer to 175˚C
2. Break your egg into a small bowl and beat it
3. Add the bread crumbs and continue whisking while adding the vegetable oil. It should take several minutes for everything to be combined but still feel loose
4. Take your chicken pieces and dip them in your mix, making sure they are fully covered
5. You can place each piece of chicken into the air fryer. It's a good idea to place a piece of parchment in first.
6. You'll only be able to do one layer at a time, it will probably mean two lots of cooking to get all eight chicken pieces cooked
7. They need to cook for 10-12 minutes
8. Place them on a plate with some of the celery, carrots, and cucumber – all cut into pieces

Baked Potatoes

SERVES 4
PREP TIME: 2 MINUTES | TOTAL: 50 MINUTES
NET CARBS: 40G | PROTEIN: 5G | FIBRE: 5G | FAT: 2G
KCAL: 206

Everyone loves baked potatoes. You may think they taste great when done in the oven but wait until you try them in the air fryer!

INGREDIENTS

- 4 good-sized baking potatoes
- 1 tsp vegetable oil of your choice
- 250g grated cheese – your choice although cheddar is always a good option
- 50g butter
- 1 large tin baked beans

INSTRUCTIONS

1. The first step, as always, is to preheat your air dryer. Set it to 200°C
2. Now scrub each of your potatoes. You can do this by hand or with a small clean scrubbing brush
3. Use some kitchen towel to dry the potatoes
4. Put the vegetable oil on a saucer and then take some in your hands and rub it into each of the potatoes
5. If you wish, add some salt and pepper to the skin of the potato as well
6. Place the potatoes in your air fryer and cook for 45 minutes. It's a good idea to turn them over halfway through. You'll need tongs for this
7. Remove and place them on a plate
8. Cut them open, and place a quarter of the butter in each one, followed by grated cheese and then baked beans.
9. Enjoy

Chicken & Chorizo Jamboree

SERVES 4
PREP TIME: 10 MINUTES | TOTAL: 35 MINUTES
NET CARBS: 64G | PROTEIN: 30G | FIBRE: 2G | FAT: 10G
KCAL: 445

INGREDIENTS

- 2 chicken breasts – you'll need to chop them
- 1 onion finely sliced
- 1 red pepper – chopped
- 2 crushed garlic cloves
- 75g chorizo
- 1 tablespoon olive oil
- 250g rice – white or brown
- 1 large can plum tomatoes

INSTRUCTIONS

1. Preheat your air fryer to 200°C

2. Place the chicken breasts in your air fryer basket on parchment paper and leave them to cook for 15 minutes. You can turn them halfway through

3. Separately, put the rice in boiling water and let it simmer for 20 minutes

4. While this is happening, place all the other ingredients, the onion, red pepper, garlic, and plum tomatoes, along with the chorizo, into a frying pan. You'll want to put the olive oil in first to prevent these from sticking

5. Heat this mixture on the stove for 10 minutes to ensure all the vegetables are browned

6. When everything is cooked, drain the rice, and add the onion mixture to the rice in a pan. Chop the chicken breasts into small pieces and add them to the pan

7. Keep it on the stove for a few moments to ensure it is all piping hot. Then, serve

Tender Chicken

SERVES 4
PREP TIME: 25 MINUTES | TOTAL: 40 MINUTES
NET CARBS: 6G | PROTEIN: 29G | FIBRE: 1G | FAT: 14G
KCAL: 256

INGREDIENTS

- 250g bread crumbs
- 2 potatoes peeled and chopped into small cubes
- 150g crackers crushed into crumbs
- 100g parmesan cheese – make sure it's grated
- 4 pieces of lean bacon, cook them under the grill then crumble them
- 50g butter – melted
- 500g chicken breasts – cut into bite-sized pieces
- 1 tbsp sour cream
- Salt and pepper to taste
- Dried herbs as desired for flavour

INSTRUCTIONS

1. Turn your air fryer on and set it to 200°C
2. In a bowl mix together your bread crumbs, potato cubes, crumbled crackers, grated parmesan, and the bacon
3. P Separately, mix your butter and sour cream together
4. Take each chicken piece and soak it in the butter mix before rolling it in the bread crumb mix
5. Place the chicken pieces in the air fryer basket, ensuring they don't touch each other. It will take two or three batches to cook them all
6. Cook the chicken in the air fryer for 7 minutes then flip them and cook for another 7 minutes
7. Serve with your desired side

Chicken Taquitos

SERVES 4
PREP TIME: 10 MINUTES | TOTAL: 30 MINUTES
NET CARBS: 18G | PROTEIN: 16G | FIBRE: 4G | FAT: 24G
KCAL: 364

INGREDIENTS

- 4 chicken breasts, cooked and grated
- 200g cheddar cheese also grated
- 3 tbsp cream cheese
- 8 tortillas
- Salt and pepper to taste
- 4 tbsp red enchilada sauce
- 150g sour cream
- Little olive oil

INSTRUCTIONS

1. Start by heating your air fryer to 210°C
2. Now mix your cream cheese with the sour cream and red enchilada sauce
3. Add a little salt and pepper if desired
4. Tip the grated chicken and cheese into the mix and make sure everything is well-mixed
5. Separate your mixture into eight equal portions and fill each tortilla, roll them up and secure them with a cocktail stick
6. Use a brush to coat the top with olive oil and then place them in the air fryer basket
7. Remember to leave space around the tortilla, it will take two or three batches depending on the size of your air fryer
8. Cook for 12 minutes, they should go golden
9. Remove from the air fryer and repeat with the next batch
10. Serve by themselves of with a salad for a delicious and healthy lunch

Squash Soup

SERVES 4
PREP TIME: 15 MINUTES | TOTAL: 25 MINUTES
NET CARBS: 36G | PROTEIN: 5G | FIBRE: 7G | FAT: 16G
KCAL: 280

INGREDIENTS

- 1kg butternut squash – you'll need to peel it and then cut it into cubes
- 2 carrots, topped and tailed then peeled and cut into cubes
- 1 onion, peeled and roughly chopped
- 4 garlic cloves crushed
- 4 tbsp olive oil
- Salt and pepper to taste
- Herbs and spices as desired, such as thyme and paprika

INSTRUCTIONS

1. Turn the air fryer on to 200°C
2. Find a mixing bowl and put the squash in with the carrots, add your onions and garlic along with two tablespoons of your olive oil
3. Add salt and pepper, as well as any herbs or spices you desire
4. Put the mixture into your air fryer basket and place it in the air fryer for 30 minutes, give the basket a shake every ten minutes
5. Move the cooked mixture into a blender and add 200ml of water
6. Blend until its smooth
7. You can serve straight away while it's still warm. It's perfect with fresh bread

Stuffed Chicken

SERVES 4
PREP TIME: 10 MINUTES | TOTAL: 25 MINUTES
NET CARBS: 7G | PROTEIN: 43G | FIBRE: 2G | FAT: 19G
KCAL: 380

INGREDIENTS

- 4 large pieces of chicken breast – make sure there are no bones and the skin is removed
- 50g goats cheese - crumbled
- 4 slices of ham
- 300g green beans – frozen or fresh
- 2 cloves of garlic – peeled and sliced
- 4 tbsp green pesto
- Salt and pepper to taste
- Olive oil

INSTRUCTIONS

1. Set the temperature on your air fryer to 180°C and let it warm
2. Take each chicken breast and slice it down the length of it. Don't go all the way through, just go as far as you can
3. Lay a coating of green pesto inside each chicken breast
4. Sprinkle the goat's cheese on top of the pesto, then close the chicken
5. Season the chicken by rolling it in olive oil and adding a little salt and pepper
6. Take a slice of ham and wrap it around the chicken breast, repeat with the other pieces of chicken
7. Lay the chicken into the air fryer basket and place them in the air fryer
8. Cook for 6 minutes
9. Now add the green beans and drizzle a small amount of oil on them
10. Cook for another 6 minutes until the chicken is cooked through, which means not pink on the inside

Med Magic Chicken

SERVES 4
PREP TIME: 10 MINUTES | TOTAL: 30 MINUTES
NET CARBS: 53G | PROTEIN: 43G | FIBRE: 5G | FAT: 10G
KCAL: 475

INGREDIENTS

- 500g chicken breasts – make sure there are no bones or skin
- 250g cherry tomatoes
- 1 onion peeled and finely chopped
- 300g couscous
- 1 tbsp olive oil
- Salt and pepper to taste
- 1 tbsp lemon juice
- 1 tsp dried oregano

INSTRUCTIONS

1. Preheat your air fryer to 200°C
2. Find a mixing bowl and add your chicken, you'll need to cut it into small pieces first
3. Add the oil and your oregano then make sure the chicken is well coated
4. Add the onion, cherry tomatoes, and any salt and pepper you desire, and gently mix it all
5. Place the mixture in the base of your air fryer, ensuring it's only one layer thick
6. Cook for 15-20 minutes, the chicken should go a golden brown
7. Separately prepare the couscous as per the instructions on the packet then mix it with the lemon juice
8. Spoon the couscous onto plates and layer the chicken across the top
9. Add any additional seasoning or sides and enjoy

Crispy Chickpeas

SERVES 2
PREP TIME: 20 MINUTES | TOTAL: 45 MINUTES
NET CARBS: 10G | PROTEIN: 25G | FIBRE: 9G | FAT: 26G
KCAL: 412

INGREDIENTS

- 600g chickpeas – the canned variety is a good choice
- 2 tbsp olive oil
- Salt and pepper to taste

INSTRUCTIONS

1. Turn your air fryer on and allow it to preheat to 210°C
2. While this is happening drain the chick peas from the cans and rinse them with tap water – use a colander to minimize water left behind
3. Pat the chickpeas dry with a clean towel or kitchen towel
4. Place a piece of parchment in the bottom of your air fryer basket, if you're using an air fryer oven then this isn't necessary
5. Put the dry chick peas in a bowl with the oil and salt and pepper
6. Mix them thoroughly then cover the bottom of your air fryer basket or place them on the baking tray
7. Cook for 30 minutes in your air fryer to get crispy chickpeas that taste delicious
8. You can add them to an air-fried cheese toasty to create a delicious lunch
9. If you want to try something different change what you toss them in, such as honey and sesame seeds

Classic Eggplant Parmesan

SERVES 4
PREP TIME: 20 MINUTES | TOTAL: 40 MINUTES
NET CARBS: 50G | PROTEIN: 23G | FIBRE: 8G | FAT: 22G
KCAL: 485

INGREDIENTS

- 2200g flour – you can choose your preferred variety
- 1 egg
- 1 egg white
- 100g parmesan cheese, grated
- 1 aubergine
- 1tbsp olive oil
- 1 garlic clove crushed
- Salt and pepper to taste
- 1 large tin ravioli
- 1 jar marinara sauce

INSTRUCTIONS

1. Preheat your air fryer to 220°C
2. Spread your flour onto a plate
3. In one bowl beat your egg
4. In a separate bowl mix the parmesan, garlic, olive oil, salt, and pepper
5. Now cut your aubergine into thin strips
6. Dunk each strip in the flour and then into your egg, followed by the parmesan mixture
7. Place each piece of aubergine in the air fryer basket or on the tray – you'll want to line the basket with greaseproof paper first
8. Cook for 15-18 minutes, the aubergine will go golden brown
9. While it's cooking, cook your ravioli as per the instructions on the tin
10. Put the ravioli on each plate, cover it with the marinara sauce and then add the aubergine pieces
11. It tastes fantastic

Pork & Ginger Meatballs

SERVES 4
PREP TIME: 20 MINUTES | TOTAL: 25 MINUTES
NET CARBS: 48G | PROTEIN: 26G | FIBRE: 2G | FAT: 31G
KCAL: 620

INGREDIENTS

- ♦ 1 egg
- ♦ 1 tbsp grated ginger
- ♦ 2 tsp lemon zest or juice
- ♦ 1 onion, peeled and finely chopped
- ♦ 2 tbsp honey
- ♦ 1 tsp fish sauce
- ♦ 1 clove garlic crushed
- ♦ 1 chilli pepper - deseeded and finely sliced
- ♦ 500g ground pork

1. Heat your air fryer to 200°C
2. Find a mixing bowl and place your egg, lemon zest, honey, fish sauce, and a little salt – then use an electric whisk to blend for at least a minute
3. Now add the ginger, onions, and garlic, and mix thoroughly before adding the pork and your chilli pepper
4. Once fully mixed take a handful of the mixture and create a meatball shape
5. Line the basket of your air fryer with greaseproof paper
6. Put each meatball into the fryer, keeping a space between each one, the exact amount you make will depend on what size you make the meatballs
7. Cook for 10 minutes, they should go brown
8. It's advisable to serve them with noodles and enjoy them straight away

DINNER SUGGESTIONS

Chicken Thighs

SERVES 4
PREP TIME: 5 MINUTES | TOTAL: 30 MINUTES
NET CARBS: 0G | PROTEIN: 8G | FIBRE: 2G | FAT: 5G
KCAL: 88

INGREDIENTS

- 4 chicken thighs
- 1 tsp paprika
- 1 tsp olive oil
- ½ tsp mixed herbs
- Optional pinch of garlic granules

INSTRUCTIONS

1. Place the paprika in a bowl and add the herbs and garlic granules. You can also use finely chopped or minced fresh garlic. Mix them together
2. Add a pinch of salt and pepper if you wish for flavour
3. Rub your chicken thighs in the olive oil. It's usually easier to pour the oil onto a plate to do this.
4. Troll the chicken thighs in the paprika and garlic mix
5. Preheat your air fryer to 180°C
6. Put chicken in the basket and cook for 10 minutes
7. Turn over and cook for another 10 minutes
8. Check the juices run clear by putting a knife in the thickest part of the thigh. Then serve with a nice salad

Pecan Pork Chops

SERVES 4
PREP TIME: 10 MINUTES | TOTAL: 25 MINUTES
NET CARBS: 6G | PROTEIN: 31G | FIBRE: 4G | FAT: 39G
KCAL: 487

This is actually a keto-friendly recipe and delicious regardless of whether you are maintaining a keto diet or not.

INGREDIENTS

- ♦ 4 pork chops – best with bone in
- ♦ 1 egg
- ♦ 300g raw pecans – finely chopped
- ♦ ½ tsp cinnamon
- ♦ Pinch ground cardamom
- ♦ 1 tsp ground cloves
- ♦ Pinch of finely chopped parsley
- ♦ Little cooking oil or spray
- ♦ Salt and pepper if desired

INSTRUCTIONS

1. The first step is to set the air dryer to 200°C and allow it to warm up
2. In a bowl, put your cinnamon, cloves, cardamom, and salt and pepper if desired. Mix them together and then add the egg. Continue mixing until they are fully blended
3. Place the raw chopped pecans onto a separate plate
4. Take your first pork chop and dip it into the egg mix. Make sure it is completely covered. Then, dip it into the pecan pieces. Again, make sure it is completely covered
5. Place the pork chop in your air fryer basket. It's a good idea to line the basket with parchment paper first
6. Repeat for the other pork chops
7. Put the basket into your air fryer and let the pork cook for 12 minutes. You'll need to turn them over halfway through. They should not be pink in the middle
8. Serve with your choice of garnish or air-fried chips

Air Fried Chips

SERVES 4
PREP TIME: 10 MINUTES | TOTAL: 35 MINUTES
NET CARBS: 24G | PROTEIN: 3G | FIBRE: 3G | FAT: 3G
KCAL: 140

These are perfect to accompany any of the meat recipes in this book or you can simply have them by themselves. They are particularly good covered in cheese

INGREDIENTS

♦ 1kg potatoes – any brand will do
♦ 1 tablespoon of olive oil – you can use other oils but olive oil is the healthiest
♦ Any garnish you desire

INSTRUCTIONS

1. Preheat your air fryer to 200°C
2. Start by peeling your potatoes, it's best to do this after dipping them in water
3. Once you've peeled them give them a good wash
4. Cut the potatoes into rectangular batons. You can square all the sides to get perfect batons on settle for imperfect ones with less wastage. Either is fine
5. Place the potato pieces into your air fryer – it doesn't matter if they are touching or on top of each other
6. Sprinkle the oil over the potato pieces and toss them in the basket to give them all a coating of oil
7. Lower the basket into the air fryer and cook for 20-25 minutes until they are cooked properly
8. Serve, add salt or any other garnish, and enjoy

Aubergine Parmesan

SERVES 4
PREP TIME: 15 MINUTES | TOTAL: 35 MINUTES
NET CARBS: 36G | PROTEIN: 24G | FIBRE: 2G | FAT: 16G
KCAL: 377

INGREDIENTS

- 250g bread crumbs
- 125g grated parmesan cheese
- 2 eggs
- 1 aubergine - sliced
- 8 slices mozzarella
- 1 jar marinara sauce
- Pinch of basil, garlic powder, onion powder, and Italian seasoning
- 250g flour
- Salt and pepper to taste

INSTRUCTIONS

1. Preheat your air fryer to 185°C
2. Mix your bread crumbs with the garlic, basil, onion, and Italian seasoning. Add in the parmesan cheese and make sure it's all blended
3. Put your flour in a separate bowl
4. Beat the eggs and place them in another bowl
5. Take the first slice of your aubergine and dip it in the flour, then the beaten eggs, and finally in the breadcrumbs. Make sure the aubergine is completely covered at each stage
6. After coating leave the aubergine on a plate for five minutes
7. Place the aubergine pieces in your air fryer and make sure they don't touch each other.
8. Cook for 15 minutes, turning them over halfway through
9. Remove from the air fryer and put on a plate, place some marinara sauce on each slice and a slice of mozzarella. Put them back in the air fryer for 1-2 minutes and then serve

Rib Eye

SERVES 2
PREP TIME: 2 HOURS | TOTAL: 20 MINUTES
NET CARBS: 8G | PROTEIN: 44G | FIBRE: 2G | FAT: 49G
KCAL: 652

What could be better than an air-fired rib-eye steak? It's delicious and surprisingly healthy

INGREDIENTS

- 2 rib-eye steaks - they should be approximately 1 ½ inches thick
- 2 tablespoons grill seasoning
- 250ml soy sauce – the reduced sodium option is better for you
- 1 125ml olive oil

INSTRUCTIONS

1. The first step is to place the rib eye steaks in a sealable bag with the soy sauce, olive oil, and seasoning. You'll want to seal the bag and give it a good shake to ensure the steaks are coated in the mixture
2. Leave this meat in the bag to marinate for two hours
3. After two hours take the steaks out of the bag and place them on a clean surface. You'll want to use some kitchen towel to pat both sides and remove excess oil
4. You can discard the bag with marinade in it
5. Preheat your air fryer to 200°C and don't forget to add a tablespoon of water to the lower tray
6. Drop the steaks into the air fryer basket, ideally, it should be lined with parchment paper first
7. Cook for 16 minutes to get a medium steak, flipping halfway through. You can cook the steaks for a little less or more depending on how you like them
8. Leave them to sit for five minutes then serve them with a salad or the air-fried chips

Lemon & Pepper Shrimp

SERVES 2
PREP TIME: 10 MINUTES | TOTAL: 20 MINUTES
NET CARBS: 15G | PROTEIN: 16G | FIBRE: 1G | FAT: 18G
KCAL: 405

INGREDIENTS

- 250g fresh shrimp – already peeled
- 2 tablespoons lemon juice
- 2 tablespoons olive oil
- As much or little salt and pepper as you wish

INSTRUCTIONS

1. Preheat the air fryer to 220°C
2. Put your shrimp in a sellable bag
3. Add the lemon juice, oil, and as much salt and pepper as you like to the bag
4. Gently shake the bag to ensure the shrimp are coated in the ingredients
5. Slide them out of the bag and place the shrimp into the air fryer basket
6. Cook the shrimp for 9 minutes, gently tossing them halfway through
7. Remove, serve, and enjoy
8. Lemon and pepper shrimp go exceptionally well with air-fried chips

Orange Chicken

SERVES 4
PREP TIME: 15 MINUTES | TOTAL: 15 MINUTES
NET CARBS: 46G | PROTEIN: 75G | FIBRE: 4G | FAT: 15G
KCAL: 630

INGREDIENTS

- 400g chicken breast
- 2 tablespoons cornflour
- 150ml orange juice
- 1 tbsp soy sauce
- 1 tbsp rice wine vinegar
- Pinch ground ginger
- Pinch red pepper flakes
- 1 orange – you just need the zest
- 2 tsp cornflour

INSTRUCTIONS

1. Start by preheating your air fryer to 220°C

2. While it's warming cut the chicken into small pieces, ideally cubes around 1 inch in size. It's best if all the pieces are roughly the same size

3. Place the chicken pieces into a bowl with the cornflour

4. Mix the two ingredients together to ensure the chicken is fully coated. Note, it should be a light coating, not a heavy one. It can help to use half the cornflour first and add more if needed

5. Drop the chicken into your air fryer basket and place the basket into the air fryer for 9 minutes – you'll want to shake the basket while it's cooking

6. While the chicken is cooking put the orange juice, brown sugar, soy sauce, ginger, orange zest, red pepper flakes, and rice wine vinegar in a small pan and put it on the stove

7. The mixture should be left to simmer for 5 minutes

8. Mix the rest of the cornflour with some water to make a paste. Add this to the sauce gradually. It will thicken it

9. Take the chicken out of the air fryer when it's ready and combine it with the sauce. Serve straightaway

Chicken Fajitas

SERVES 4
PREP TIME: 10 MINUTES | TOTAL: 20 MINUTES
NET CARBS: 7G | PROTEIN: 19G | FIBRE: 2G | FAT: 6G
KCAL: 155

INGREDIENTS

- 4 tortillas
- 4 skinless chicken breasts – cut into small strips
- 1 red or yellow pepper - chopped
- 1 onion – finely sliced
- 1 tbsp olive oil
- 1 tbsp chilli powder
- 2tsp lime juice
- Pinch of cumin
- Salt and pepper as desired

INSTRUCTIONS

1. Preheat the air fryer to 180°C
2. Find a medium-sized bowl and put all your ingredients into it
3. Blend the ingredients to ensure they are evenly distributed
4. Take a tortilla and fold it in half, press the ends together
5. Fill the tortilla with the ingredients and place it carefully in your air fryer basket
6. Repeat for the other tortillas
7. Put the basket into the air fryer and cook for 10-15 minutes, make sure the chicken is properly cooked all the way through
8. Remove the fajitas and serve with your choice of dressing or side dish

Meatloaf

SERVES 4
PREP TIME: 10 MINUTES | TOTAL: 45 MINUTES
NET CARBS: 13G | PROTEIN: 14G | FIBRE: 1G | FAT: 9G
KCAL: 189

The air fryer is the perfect way to get meatloaf crispy on the outside and still moist in the middle. It can be served with an array of vegetables or the air-fried chips mentioned earlier

INGREDIENTS

- 1kg ground beef
- 2 eggs
- 125ml milk
- 300g breadcrumbs
- 1 packet of meatloaf seasoning
- 1 ½ tbsp Worcestershire sauce
- 200ml tomato ketchup
- 200g sugar
- 1 tbsp mustard

INSTRUCTIONS

1. The first step is to turn your air fryer on and preheat it to 175°C
2. Mix the ground beef with the beaten eggs in a bowl
3. Slowly add the seasoning, milk, bread crumbs, and 1 tablespoon of the Worcestershire sauce. Mix it all thoroughly
4. It should be solid enough to form into the shape of a meatloaf
5. Place it into the air fryer basket and lower the basket into the air fryer
6. Cook for 25 minutes
7. Separately, mix the tomato ketchup with half a tablespoon of Worcestershire sauce, the sugar, and the mustard
8. Once the meatloaf has cooked for 25 minutes, remove it from the air fryer
9. Cover the meatloaf with the tomato ketchup mixture and put it back in the air fryer for another 5 minutes
10. Serve by itself or with a selection of vegetables and enjoy

Country Fried Steak

SERVES 2
PREP TIME: 15 MINUTES | TOTAL: 40 MINUTES
NET CARBS: 32G | PROTEIN: 23G | FIBRE: 2G | FAT: 28G
KCAL: 280

INGREDIENTS

- ◆ 400g steak of your choice – you'll need to cut it into sections
- ◆ 100g flour
- ◆ 1 egg
- ◆ 1 tsp garlic powder or 2 crushed cloves
- ◆ 50ml water
- ◆ Salt and pepper to taste
- ◆ 1 tsp paprika
- ◆ 1 tsp ground pepper

INSTRUCTIONS

1. Start by turning on your air fryer, set the temperature to 175°C
2. Take the steak, already cut into 4-6 pieces, and tenderise it – you can use a mallet
3. In one bowl mix your flour, garlic, paprika, pepper, and any salt or pepper
4. Separately, beat the egg into the water
5. Now take one of the steak pieces and roll it in the flour mixture
6. Transfer it to the egg mixture and then back to the flour mixture, it should be coated all over
7. Repeat with the other steak pieces
8. Line your air fryer basket with greaseproof paper and place the steak pieces in the basket, make sure you leave a space between each one
9. Cook for 15 minutes, you'll need to turn them over half way through the cooking process
10. You can check they are done with an internal temperature thermometer, it should show at least 70°C
11. It's best to let the steak rest for a few minutes before serving

Delicious Fried Cod

SERVES 2
PREP TIME: 10 MINUTES | TOTAL: 20 MINUTES
NET CARBS: 3G | PROTEIN: 42G | FIBRE: 1G | FAT: 8G
KCAL: 302

INGREDIENTS

- 50g butter
- 2 cloves garlic- crushed
- 1 tsp lemon juice
- Fresh dill – chopped into small sections
- 2 cod fillets

INSTRUCTIONS

1. Step one is to set the temperature on your air fryer to 175˚C and leave it to heat up
2. In a bowl mix your butter with crushed garlic and lemon juice. Once mixed sprinkle in the finely cut dill
3. Assess your cod pieces. If they will fir in the air fryer as they are then leave them whole, if not, cut them into sections to ensure you can cook all the cod at the same time
4. Cover the cod in the butter mixture, it's easiest to dip the cod in the bowl and roll it around
5. Place some greaseproof paper in the bottom of your air fryer basket
6. Add the cod to the basket, making sure the pieces aren't touching each other
7. Cook for 10 minutes, turning them over halfway through
8. Enjoy with your chosen side

Cajun Salmon

SERVES 2
PREP TIME: 10 MINUTES | TOTAL: 20 MINUTES
NET CARBS: 4G | PROTEIN: 34G | FIBRE: 3G | FAT: 19G
KCAL: 327

INGREDIENTS

- 2 salmon fillets – it's best to choose ones that still have the skin on
- 1 tbsp Cajun spices
- 1 tbsp brown sugar
- Little cooking spray
- Piece of greaseproof paper

INSTRUCTIONS

1. As always, start by preheating your air fryer. In this case, set it to 200°C
2. Now take your salmon fillets. You can keep them whole if they will fit into your air fryer. If not, cut them into sections
3. Rinse the salmon fillets and dry them with a kitchen towel
4. In a bowl, mix your brown sugar and Cajun spices, you can add extra spices or salt and pepper if you desire
5. Lay the sugar and Cajun spice mixture across a plate or the countertop
6. Roll each piece of salmon in the spices, pressing firmly to ensure they attach properly
7. Place the greaseproof paper in the air fryer basket and lightly spray the basket
8. Add the salmon pieces
9. Cook for 8 minutes and then leave it to sit for 2 minutes before serving. It's that simple to make a healthy and delicious salmon dish

Stuffed Turkey Breast

SERVES 6
PREP TIME: 10 MINUTES | TOTAL: 50 MINUTES
NET CARBS: 0G | PROTEIN: 40G | FIBRE: 2G | FAT: 10G
KCAL: 263

INGREDIENTS

- 1.25 kg turkey breast – preferably with the bone in and the skin still on
- 50g butter
- 2 cloves crushed garlic
- 1 tsp ground rosemary
- A handful of chives chopped into small pieces
- Salt and pepper as desired

INSTRUCTIONS

1. Turn the air fryer on and set it to 175°C, allow it to reach this temperature before you place anything in it
2. Put your rosemary in a bowl with the garlic, chives, and any salt and pepper you want. Then, add the butter and mash the mixture together, ensuring it's fully blended
3. Rinse the turkey breast with water and dry it with kitchen towel before rubbing the butter mixture across the breast, make sure you get some under the skin
4. Put greaseproof paper in the air fryer basket than add the turkey
5. The skin should face down as you cook it for 20 minutes
6. Turn the turkey over and continue cooking for another 10-15 minutes, an internal thermometer should read 74°C or higher
7. Once cooked put the turkey on a plate and let it sit for ten minutes while you decide what to serve it with

Fish Tacos

SERVES 4
PREP TIME: 15 MINUTES | TOTAL: 30 MINUTES
NET CARBS: 43G | PROTEIN: 33G | FIBRE: 3G | FAT: 7G
KCAL: 361

INGREDIENTS

- 1 standard tin black beans (approx. 500g)
- 300g sweetcorn
- 500g tilapia fillets
- 1 tbsp olive oil
- 1 tbsp lime juice – or lemon if you prefer
- 4 medium-sized tortillas
- Salt and pepper to taste
- Seasoning of your choice

INSTRUCTIONS

1. Preheat your air fryer to 200°C
2. Drain and then rinse the black beans before putting them in a bowl
3. Add the sweetcorn, (after draining), and the olive oil, along with the lime juice and any salt and pepper you want. Mix until thoroughly blended
4. Put your tilapia fillets on a chopping board and use kitchen towel to ensure they are completely dry – dab, don't rub
5. Spray the fillets with a little cooking oil and then sprinkle your chosen seasoning across them. Blackened seasoning is a good choice but anything tastes great
6. Turn the fillets over and repeat with the other side
7. Put the fish fillets in your air fryer basket, making sure there is a space around all of them
8. Cook for 2 minutes before turning them over and cooking for another two minutes
9. Repeat as many times as necessary until all the fillets are cooked
10. Now add your bean mixture to the air fryer and cook for 10 minutes, you'll want to lightly toss the mixture part way through the cooking process
11. Put your fish into the tortillas and add the bean mixture, now you're ready to taste your fish tacos

Chilli Burritos

SERVES 10
PREP TIME: 10 MINUTES | TOTAL: 30 MINUTES
NET CARBS: 19G | PROTEIN: 13G | FIBRE: 3G | FAT: 5G
KCAL: 180

INGREDIENTS

- 500g pulled pork – chopped as finely as possible
- 1 jar salsa – you choose how hot you want it to be
- 50g cheddar cheese - grated
- 10 standard flour tortillas
- 1 tbsp chilli powder – adjust to taste
- Cooking oil in spray bottle

INSTRUCTIONS

1. Your air fryer needs to be preheated to 200°C
2. In a bowl mix your pork, salsa, chilli powder, and grated cheese. Mix thoroughly
3. Take one of the tortillas and add a spoonful of the mixture. It's easier to create the pocket first by folding each end
4. Repeat the process with the other 9 tortillas – if you want to be more generous with the filling, you'll need fewer tortillas
5. Spray your air fryer basket with the cooking spray, this prevents them from sticking and improves the crispiness
6. Add as many of the burritos as you can, making sure there is a gap around each one
7. Cook for 6 minutes then remove and repeat the cooking process with the next batch
8. Once they are all cooked, enjoy

Classic Cheeseburgers

SERVES 2
PREP TIME: 10 MINUTES | TOTAL: 30 MINUTES
NET CARBS: 42G | PROTEIN: 54G | FIBRE: 5G | FAT: 47G
KCAL: 822

INGREDIENTS

- 500g ground beef
- 4 slices of cheddar cheese
- 2 burger buns – brioche is best but regular ones will do
- 1 slice of white bread
- 2 tbsp milk
- 1 tsp garlic powder or one crushed clove
- Salt and pepper to taste

INSTRUCTIONS

1. Fire up the air fryer and set the temperature to 175°C
2. Take your slice of white bread and remove the crust. Then, break the bread into pieces, to should be almost like crumbs
3. Put the bread in a bowl and mix in the garlic, any slat and pepper, and the milk
4. Now add the ground beef and blend the ingredients together
5. You should be able to scoop half of the mixture out and make it into a burger shape
6. Repeat with the other half
7. Push your thumb into the middle of each burger, making an indentation stops them from puffing while cooking
8. Lightly spray the air fryer basket and place both the burgers in it
9. Drop it into the air fryer and let the burgers cook for 10 minutes, flip them over and let them cook for another 10 minutes
10. You can reduce the cooking time to 8 minutes per side if you prefer them less well-done
11. Remove the burgers and put them in the brioche bun with two slices of cheddar on top of each burger

Ranch Chops

SERVES 4
PREP TIME: 5 MINUTES | TOTAL: 25 MINUTES
NET CARBS: 1G | PROTEIN: 41G | FIBRE: 1G | FAT: 9G
KCAL:260

INGREDIENTS

- 4 pork chops – preferably boneless and approximately one inch thick
- 2 tbsp dry ranch dressing or a similar ranch dressing of your choice
- Oil cooking spray
- Silver foil

INSTRUCTIONS

1. Your air fryer should be preheated to 200°C, it's best to turn it on before you do anything else
2. Lay your pork chops on the side and spray them with the cooking spray. They only need a little oil on each one
3. Spread the ranch seasoning across the chops then turn them and repeat the process with the other side
4. Leave the chops to rest at room temperature for at least 10 minutes
5. Lightly spray the air fryer basket and place the chops in it
6. Make sure they are not touching each other
7. Cook for 5 minutes then turn them over before cooking for another 5 minutes
8. Transfer them to a plate that you've' covered in tin foil, leave them to rest for 5 minutes then you can serve them by themselves or with a nice salad

DESERT DELIGHTS

Cinnamon & Sugar Doughnuts

MAKES 10
PREP TIME: 15 MINUTES | TOTAL: 15 MINUTES
NET CARBS: 44G | PROTEIN: 4G | FIBRE: 1G | FAT: 10G
KCAL: 276

INGREDIENTS

- 200g sugar
- 45g butter
- 2 egg yolks
- 325g flour
- 1 ½ tsp baking powder
- 60g sour cream
- 1 tsp cinnamon

INSTRUCTIONS

1. Start by combining 125g of sugar with the butter. Make it crumbly then add the egg yolks
2. Use half the flour and a third of the sour cream, put them into the mixture and blend. Slowly add the rest of the flour and sour cream
3. Put this dough in the refrigerator
4. Mix the cinnamon and 75g of sugar together
5. Roll the dough out until it's 2cm thick. Cut large circles to create your doughnuts. Remove a small circle in the centre of each
6. Heat your fryer to 175°C
7. Brush the doughnuts lightly with melted butter
8. Put in the air fryer basket and cook for 8 minutes – dip them immediately in the cinnamon mix and allow to cool before enjoying

Traditional Apple Pie

SERVES 4
PREP TIME: 30 MINUTES | TOTAL: 45 MINUTES
NET CARBS: 60G | PROTEIN: 3G | FIBRE: 1G | FAT: 2ÇG
KCAL: 497

INGREDIENTS

- 50g butter
- 75g sugar – preferably brown sugar
- I tsp ground cinnamon
- 2 apples – cut into small pieces
- 2 tsp water
- 1 tsp cornflour
- 200g pastry – from a packet or homemade
- Cooking oil in a spray bottle
- 125g powdered sugar or icing sugar
- Few drops of milk
- 1 tsp grapeseed oil

INSTRUCTIONS

1. Start by preheating your air fryer to 195°C
2. Mix your apple pieces with the brown sugar and cinnamon. Put them in a pan and warm slowly on the stove until the apples have softened
3. Separately put the cornflour in your water and allow it to dissolve
4. Add the cornflour mixture to your apple mixture to help the sauce thicken
5. After a minute remove it from the heat and leave to cool
6. Roll out your pastry and cut eight equal-sized rectangles out of it
7. Use a brush to wet the outer edges of each rectangle
8. Place a large spoonful of your mixture on four of the rectangles
9. Roll the other four rectangles again to make them slightly larger
10. Put the larger four on top of the filling and crimp the edges together
11. Add four small slits to the top piece of pastry
12. Spray the inside of your air fryer basket with the cooking oil and then put two of the apple pies in the basket
13. Coat the tops with some grapeseed oil
14. Lower the basket into the air fryer and cook for 8 minutes – they should be golden brown
15. Repeat for the other two pies
16. You can enjoy them like this or mix the powdered sugar with milk to create a glaze across the top of the apple pie

Coated Oreos

CREATES 9 SERVINGS
PREP TIME: 5 MINUTES | TOTAL: 15 MINUTES
NET CARBS: 14G | PROTEIN: 1G | FIBRE: 1G | FAT: 2G
KCAL: 77

Who doesn't love Oreos? This recipe makes them even better!

INGREDIENTS

- 250ml pancake mix – from a bottle or homemade
- 75ml water
- 9 Oreos
- Confectioners' sugar
- Cooking oil in a spray bottle

INSTRUCTIONS

1. Preheat your air fryer to 200˚C
2. While it is heating remove the basket and line it with parchment paper
3. Put the pancake mix and water in a bowl and mix thoroughly
4. Put the cookies into the pancake mix and make sure they are fully coated
5. Put them in the air fryer basket but don't let them touch each other
6. Cook for 8 minutes, flipping partway through
7. Remove and sprinkle the confectioners' sugar over them
8. Allow to cool before eating

Coconut Macaroons

MAKES 36 MACAROONS
PREP TIME: 15 MINUTES | TOTAL: 1HR 40 MINUTES
NET CARBS: 12G | PROTEIN: 1G | FIBRE: 1G | FAT: 6G
KCAL: 103

INGREDIENTS

- 400g sweetened flaked coconut
- 3300ml condensed milk
- Pinch of salt
- 1 tsp vanilla extract
- 2 egg whites
- 200g dark chocolate

INSTRUCTIONS

1. Start by preheating your air fryer to 160°C
2. Lift the basket out first and add a piece of parchment paper to the bottom of the basket
3. Mix your coconut, condensed milk, vanilla essence, and salt if desired in a bowl
4. Separately beat your egg whites, they should be at room temperature. It should take approximately one and a half minutes to make the egg whites stiff
5. Fold the egg whites into the coconut mixture
6. Use a tablespoon to create mounds on the parchment paper in your air fryer basket. You should get 6 mounds at a time
7. Cook for 8-10 minutes until golden brown
8. Place the cooked macaroons on a wire rack while you cook the rest
9. Melt the chocolate in the microwave or over the stove
10. Dip the base of your cooked macaroons into the melted chocolate and then place them on more parchment paper to set. This takes about 30 minutes
11. Enjoy

Triple Chocolate Cookies

MAKES 36 COOKIES
PREP TIME: 15 MINUTES | TOTAL: 25 MINUTES
NET CARBS: 2.8G | PROTEIN: 11.4G | FIBRE: 6.9G | FAT: 25G
KCAL: 302

INGREDIENTS

- 500g quick-cook porridge oats
- 375g flour
- 125g cocoa powder
- 1 tsp baking soda
- 1 tsp salt
- 300g butter
- 250g brown sugar
- 250g white sugar
- 2 eggs
- 400g chocolate chips
- 1 tsp vanilla essence
- Cooking spray

INSTRUCTIONS

1. Preheat your air fryer to 175°C Spray the cooking basket with the cooking spray to help prevent food from sticking to it
2. Mix your oats with the flour, cocoa powder, and baking soda in a bowl. You can add a pinch of salt if desired
3. Separately cream the butter and both lots of sugar. It's easiest with an electric mixer
4. Blend the eggs and vanilla essence into the butter mix
5. Combine the two mixtures in one bowl
6. Add your chocolate chips and stir in, the dough will be thick at this stage
7. Put scoops of the cookie dough in your air fryer basket – don't let them touch each other
8. Cook for 6-10 minutes until they go a light golden colour
9. Move to a wire rack and cook the next batch

Banana Cake

SERVES 4
PREP TIME: 10 MINUTES | TOTAL: 40 MINUTES
NET CARBS: 57G | PROTEIN: 5G | FIBRE: 6G | FAT: 12G
KCAL: 347

INGREDIENTS

- 150g brown sugar
- 75g butter
- 1 egg
- 2 mashed bananas – it's a great way to use up bananas that are too far gone to eat
- 300g self-raising flour
- 2 tbsp honey
- Pinch cinnamon
- Cooking oil in a spray bottle

INSTRUCTIONS

1. The first step is to turn your air fryer on and set it to 160°C
2. Put the sugar and butter in a bowl and blend them with an electric whisk. This will ensure they are really smooth
3. Separately put your mushed banana, the honey and break the egg into a bowl and mix thoroughly
4. Whisk the two mixtures in one bowl, to create a smooth texture
5. Slowly add the flour and cinnamon to the mix and continue whisking to keep it all smooth
6. Move the mixture into a pan that will fit inside your air fryer basket
7. Drop the basket into the air fryer and leave it to cook for 30 minutes
8. It's best to let it cool for 15 minutes before serving

Cherry Crumble – Gluten Free!

SERVES 4
PREP TIME: 15 MINUTES | TOTAL: 1HR 10 MINUTES
NET CARBS: 76G | PROTEIN: 5G | FIBRE: 2G | FAT: 18G
KCAL: 459

INGREDIENTS

- 150g butter
- 500g cherries – or a mixture of fruits if you prefer. They'll need to be pitted
- 250g flour – for a gluten-free recipe use gluten-free flour
- 100g sugar
- 2 tbsp lemon juice
- 1 tsp vanilla essence
- 1 tsp cinnamon
- 1 tsp nutmeg

1. Start by cubing your butter and then putting it in the freezer. It should take 10-15 minutes to be firm

2. When the butter is ready turn on your air fryer and set it to 165°C

3. In a medium-sized bowl, put the cherries, 20g of sugar, and the lemon juice. Mix them well together and then put the contents into a baking dish. The dish will need to fit in your air fryer. It can be a good idea to line the dish with parchment as this reduces washing afterwards.

4. In a clean bowl, mix the flour and 60g of sugar. Then, cut in the butter until the mixture is roughly the size of peas

5. Pour this over the cherry mix

6. Separately, mix 20g sugar with the vanilla essence, cinnamon, and nutmeg. Sprinkle this over the top of the flour mix

7. Place the pan in the air fryer basket and lower it into the air fryer. It should take 25-30 minutes to lightly brown. At this stage turn off the air fryer and leave the cherry crumble in it for another 10 minutes

8. Remove and allow to cool for 5 minutes before serving

Chocolate Cake

SERVES 4
PREP TIME: 10 MINUTES | TOTAL: 25 MINUTES
NET CARBS: 26G | PROTEIN: 3G | FIBRE: 1G | FAT: 12G
KCAL: 214

INGREDIENTS

- 125g sugar
- 75g butter
- 1 egg
- 75g flour
- 1 tablespoon jam – your preferred flavour
- 25g cocoa powder
- Cooking oil in a spray bottle

INSTRUCTIONS

1. Turn your air fryer on and set it to 160°C – use the cooking oil spray to coat a fluted tube pan. Ideally, one that will fit inside the air fryer
2. Place the sugar and butter in a bowl, and beat them until creamy. It's faster with an electric whisk
3. Add your egg and preferred jam and mix them in to combine them fully
4. Next, put the flour and cocoa powder into the mix and continue to blend
5. Once finished, pour it into the pan and make sure the mixture is level
6. Put it in the air fryer and cook for 15 minutes
7. Let it cool for 10 minutes before you enjoy

Apple Cider Doughnut Bites

MAKES 21 DOUGHNUT BITES
PREP TIME: 10 MINUTES | TOTAL: 50 MINUTES
NET CARBS: 26G | PROTEIN: 2G | FIBRE: 1G | FAT: 3G
KCAL: 132

INGREDIENTS

Before you start make sure you have small silicon moulds. If not, you will need to order them before you can do this recipe.

- 300g flour
- 75g sugar
- 30g baking powder
- 125ml apple cider
- 1 tsp mixed spices
- 100g apple sauce
- 100g butter – preferably unsalted
- 1 egg
- 1 tsp apple cider vinegar

INSTRUCTIONS

1. Preheat your air fryer to 200˚C
2. Mix together your flour, sugar, baking powder, and spices
3. Separately mix the apple sauce with the cider and vinegar.
4. Melt the butter and add it to the apple sauce mix
5. Blend the two mixtures together a little at a time
6. Scoop some of the mixture with a large spoon or ice cream scoop and place it in the silicone mould – two scoops should fill the mould
7. Reduce the temperature in the air fryer to 175˚C and put as many moulds as you can fit in without stacking them
8. Cook for 10 minutes, turning them carefully over after 8 minutes
9. They'll need to cool on a wire rack for approximately 30 minutes before they can be eaten

Smores

SERVES 1
PREP TIME: 5 MINUTES | TOTAL: 10 MINUTES
NET CARBS: 18G | PROTEIN: 4G | FIBRE: 0G | FAT: 26G
KCAL: 150

INGREDIENTS

- Crackers – you can choose any that you like
- 1 bar of dark chocolate
- Packet of large marshmallows

INSTRUCTIONS

1. Preheat your air fryer to 170°C, make sure you remove the basket while it's heating
2. It's advisable to line the bottom of the basket with greaseproof paper, it will reduce the mess
3. Place several crackers in the bottom of your air fryer basket, make sure they aren't touching each other
4. Take one large marshmallow and break it in half, place the two halves on your cracker, you can add more if the cracker is large
5. Put 2-3 squares of dark chocolate on top of the marshmallows
6. Add another marshmallow split into two pieces
7. Put a second cracker on top
8. Repeat for as many crackers as you can fit in your air fryer basket
9. Cook them for 1-2 minutes, they will quickly melt and taste delicious

Vanilla Cinnamon Ice Cream!

SERVES 1
PREP TIME: 5 MINUTES | TOTAL: 3-4 HOURS
NET CARBS: 32G | PROTEIN: 1G | FIBRE: 0G | FAT: 35G
KCAL: 210

INGREDIENTS

- 1 scoop of vanilla ice cream per serving
- 1 tsp ground cinnamon
- 50g granola
- Additional toppings such as flavoured syrup or cherries as desired

INSTRUCTIONS

1. Find a baking tray and line it with greaseproof paper
2. Take one large scoop of ice cream, you can use different flavours if you prefer
3. Roll the ice cream into a ball and roll it across the cinnamon and granola
4. If the granola pieces are large, you can crush them first by putting them in a bag and hitting it with a rolling pin
5. Make sure the ice cream ball is fully coated before putting them on your baking tray
6. Once you've done enough balls put the tray in the freezer and leave for 3-4 hours
7. Before removing the balls, turn on your air fryer and set it to 220°C
8. Take the ice cream balls out of the freezer and put them straight into the air fryer
9. Cook for 2 minutes and enjoy with any topping you fancy. You'll be pleasantly surprised

Roasted Bananas

SERVES 1
PREP TIME: 5 MINUTES | TOTAL: 15 MINUTES
NET CARBS: 27G | PROTEIN: 1G | FIBRE: 8G | FAT: 1G
KCAL: 107

INGREDIENTS

♦ 1 banana, peeled and then
sliced into diagonal sections
♦ Cooking oil spray

INSTRUCTIONS

1. Start by preheating your air fryer to 190°C
2. Place a piece of greaseproof paper in the bottom of your air fryer basket
3. Put the pieces of banana into the basket. Remember to keep a gap around each piece
4. Lightly spray the banana pieces with your cooking oil spray
5. Drop the basket into the air fryer and cook for 5 minutes
6. Carefully turn banana pieces over before cooking for another 3 minutes
7. The banana pieces will have browned off beautiful

Nutella Turnovers

SERVES 12
PREP TIME: 10 MINUTES | TOTAL: 20 MINUTES
NET CARBS: 14G | PROTEIN: 3G | FIBRE: 2G | FAT: 11G
KCAL: 163

INGREDIENTS

- 1 sheet of puff pastry from a packet or you can make your own
- 200g chocolate spread, it doesn't have to be Nutella
- 50g hazelnuts – finely chopped then toasted
- 1 egg
- 2 tbsp water

INSTRUCTIONS

1. Start by preheating your air fryer to 200°C
2. Spread a little flour on the side to prevent the pastry from sticking. Put the pastry on the flour and roll it. You'll need to make it approximately 20x30 cm
3. Cut your pastry into twelve identically sized pieces
4. Put a teaspoon of chocolate spread on the centre of each piece
5. Sprinkle some of the toasted hazelnut pieces on top of the chocolate spread
6. Fold one of the squares in half diagonally. You'll make a triangle
7. Pinch the edges together and repeat for the other 11 squares
8. In a bowl put your egg and water, then beat them until fully blended
9. Brush the egg mixture across the top of each triangle. It helps it brown and seals the edges
10. Add the triangles to your air fryer basket, making sure they don't touch each other. You may need to do more than one batch
11. Cook for 5-7 minutes and allow them to cool for at least 5 minutes before eating

Shortbread Fries

SERVES 24
PREP TIME: 20 MINUTES | TOTAL: 30 MINUTES
NET CARBS: 12G | PROTEIN: 1G | FIBRE: 1G | FAT: 4G
KCAL: 88

INGREDIENTS

- 400g self-raising flour
- 75g sugar
- 250g butter
- 100g jam – choose your preferred flavour
- 100g lemon curd

INSTRUCTIONS

1. Turn the air fryer on and set it to 175°C
2. Place your flour and sugar in a bowl and mix them together
3. Next, add your butter and blend until you have fine crumbs. You can do this with a fork, your fingers, or a dedicated pastry blender
4. Knead the dough for several minutes
5. Spread a little flour on the side and then put your dough on it
6. Using a rolling pin flatten the mixture, you'll want it to be approximately 2cm thick
7. Now cut the rolled dough into rectangular pieces, similar to chunky fries
8. Sprinkle the fires on both sides with a little sugar
9. Place as many shortbread fries as you can in your air fryer basket, making sure they are not touching each other
10. Cook for 3-4 minutes then repeat with the rest of the shortbread fries
11. Separately push your jam through a sieve to remove all seeds and mix the results with the lemon curd. You can drizzle this over the shortbread fries or use it as a dip

Mini Cherry Pasties

SERVES 8
PREP TIME: 20 MINUTES | TOTAL: 30 MINUTES
NET CARBS: 32G | PROTEIN: 3G | FIBRE: 1G | FAT: 15G
KCAL: 279

INGREDIENTS

- 400g flour
- 200g butter
- 200g pitted cherries
- 100g sugar
- Cooking oil spray

1. Start by making your pastry. That means kneading the butter, flour and half the sugar together to create a dough, with a little water. It's best to do this with your hands

2. Sprinkle some flour on the side and roll the pastry out with a rolling pin. It should be half a centimetre thick

3. If you prefer you can purchase sweet pastry ready-made, you'll still need to roll it

4. You can now turn on your air fryer and set the temperature to 175°C

5. Cut circles in the dough approximately 8cm wide

6. In a separate bowl put the rest of your sugar and the cherries, and cut them into small pieces. You can add extra flavourings if you wish

7. In the centre of each circle place a large spoonful of the cherry mixture

8. Fold the circles in half and drizzle a small amount of water on the edges to help them bind together with a standard pasty crimped edge

9. Make a small cut on the top of the dough to prevent the pasty bubbling

10. Put as many as you can in the air fryer basket and cook for 9 minutes. Remember to leave space around them

11. Serve with cream, ice cream, or by themselves. But, remember that the insides will be very hot

Blueberry Scones

SERVES 8
PREP TIME: 15 MINUTES | TOTAL: 30 MINUTES
NET CARBS: 20G | PROTEIN: 3G | FIBRE: 2G | FAT: 4G
KCAL: 122

INGREDIENTS

- 300g self-raising flour
- 75g sugar
- 50g butter
- 1 egg
- Pinch of salt
- 150ml buttermilk – make by mixing 150ml of milk with a tbsp lemon juice and leaving at room temperature for 10 minutes
- 200g fresh blueberries
- Zest of one orange
- 1 tsp vanilla extract or flavouring

1. Start by preheating your air fryer to 180°C
2. Mix your flour with half the sugar in a bowl. Then, add a pinch of salt if desired
3. Add your butter to the flour and mix until it becomes fine breadcrumbs. It's often best to do this by hand
4. Separately, beat your egg and, once beaten, place two tablespoons of the egg in another bowl
5. Pour the larger portion of egg into the buttermilk and add your vanilla, stirring continuously while doing so
6. Fold the liquid mix into your flour using a minimal amount of stirring to ensure it's all mixed
7. Add the blueberries, they can be whole or cut into pieces
8. Put a little flour on your countertop and place the scone dough o it. Gently and carefully knead the dough to eliminate stickiness
9. Pat or roll your dough to create a circle approximately 15cm wide
10. Break the circle into 8 pieces
11. Mix the rest of the sugar with the orange zest
12. Put a little of the remaining egg on top of each of the dough pieces and then the sugar and orange mixture
13. Place them in the air fryer basket ensuring they are not touching
14. Cook for 6 minutes and repeat with the second batch if necessary

Butter Cake

SERVES 4
PREP TIME: 10 MINUTES | TOTAL: 30 MINUTES
NET CARBS: 60G | PROTEIN: 8G | FIBRE: 2G | FAT: 22G
KCAL: 470

INGREDIENTS

- 150g butter
- 150g sugar
- 1 egg
- S350g self-raising flour
- 50ml milk
- Pinch of salt if desired
- Flaked almonds or almond essence

INSTRUCTIONS

1. Before you start you need to find a cake tin that will fit into your air fryer basket
2. Turn your air fryer on and set it to 180°C
3. Put your butter and most of the sugar in a bowl and mix them together to make the buttercream, you can use an electric whisk if you prefer
4. Beat the egg into the butter and sugar
5. Add your flour, almonds, and any salt you want then mix lightly
6. Pour in the milk while stirring to create a smooth batter
7. Move the batter mixture into your baking tin and pat it all down to create an even layer
8. Cook in your air fryer for 15 minutes. You can check it's cooked by inserting a toothpick in the centre, it should come out clean
9. It's best to take the cake out of the pan straight away and let it cool on a rack for 5 minutes before serving

SIDES & SNACKS

Cauliflower pieces

SERVES 4
PREP TIME: 5 MINUTES | TOTAL: 15 MINUTES
NET CARBS: 20G | PROTEIN: 3G | FIBRE: 1G | FAT: 6G
KCAL: 147

These are surprisingly tasty and a great way to increase vegetable consumption

INGREDIENTS

- 1 large bag of frozen cauliflower pieces
- Cooking oil in a spray bottle

INSTRUCTIONS

1. Start by preheating your air fryer to 200°C
2. Open your bag of frozen cauliflower pieces and place them in the air fryer basket
3. It's essential that the cauliflower pieces don't touch each other – you'll probably need to cook the bag in batches
4. Lower the basket into the air fryer and cook for 6 minutes
5. Remove the basket, carefully turn the pieces over and put them back in the air fryer for another 3 minutes – they should be browning
6. Enjoy

Sour Cream Mushrooms

MAKES 24 MUSHROOMS
PREP TIME: 30 MINUTES | TOTAL: 45 MINUTES
NET CARBS: 2G | PROTEIN: 2G | FIBRE: 1G | FAT: 3G
KCAL: 43

INGREDIENTS

- 24 mushrooms with stem diced
- 1 yellow or orange pepper – finely chopped
- 1 onion – finely chopped
- 1 carrot – finely chopped
- 2 slices of bacon – finely chopped
- 250g grated cheese – cheddar is best but any will do
- 125g sour cream

INSTRUCTIONS

1. Start by cooking the mushrooms in a frying pan with a little oil. Add the pepper, carrot, and onion to ensure all are softened
2. Add the cheese and sour cream, blending while they heat allowing the cheese to melt
3. Turn on your air fryer and set it to 175°C
4. Place the mushrooms in the base of the air fryer basket. They should be upside down
5. Tadd a large spoonful of the mixture to the top of each mushroom – you'll probably need to cook them in batches
6. Cook for 8-10 minutes until golden brown
7. Do the next lot while enjoying the first ones

Ranch Chickpeas

SERVES 2
PREP TIME: 5 MINUTES | TOTAL: 30 MINUTES
NET CARBS: 34G | PROTEIN: 7G | FIBRE: 2G | FAT: 2G
KCAL: 177

INGREDIENTS

- 1 large can of chickpeas
- 3 tablespoons barbecue sauce
- 1 tablespoon ranch dressing or dry mix

INSTRUCTIONS

1. Start by turning your air fryer on and heating it to 175°C
2. Put some kitchen towel on your side and pour the chickpeas onto it. If the chickpeas are in brine or other liquid drain this off first
3. Use more kitchen towel to dab the chickpeas, removing as much moisture as possible
4. Transfer the chickpeas to a bowl and add your barbecue sauce
5. Add the ranch dressing and mix thoroughly
6. Line the air fryer basket with parchment paper and cover the base with chickpeas
7. Cook for 20 minutes, shaking them every 5 minutes to ensure even cooking
8. Let them cool for 5 minutes before you serve

Stuffed Mushrooms

SERVES 6
PREP TIME: 20 MINUTES | TOTAL: 35 MINUTES
NET CARBS: 4G | PROTEIN: 5G | FIBRE: 2G | FAT: 8G
KCAL: 104

INGREDIENTS

♦ 1kg button mushrooms
♦ 2 scallions
♦ 250g cream cheese

♦ 150g grated cheddar cheese
♦ Pinch of paprika

INSTRUCTIONS

1. Start by cleaning the mushrooms. It's best to do this gently with a damp cloth
2. Mince your scallions and then separate the green and white parts
3. Turn the air fryer on and set it to 180°C
4. In a bowl, mix the grated cheddar, cream cheese, paprika, and the white part of the scallions
5. Push the mixture into the button mushrooms
6. Lightly spray your air fryer basket with cooking oil to prevent the mushrooms from sticking
7. Place the stuffed mushrooms in the basket, do not stack them. You'll probably need to do two batches
8. Cook for 6-8 minutes until browning
9. Remove and sprinkle the green scallions on the mushrooms then leave them to cool for five minutes before eating

Mozzarella Sticks

SERVES 4
PREP TIME: 20 MINUTES | TOTAL: 1 HR 35 MINUTES
NET CARBS: 39G | PROTEIN: 13G | FIBRE: 1G | FAT: 7G
KCAL: 246

INGREDIENTS

- 125g flour
- 125ml water
- 100g cornflour
- 1 tbsp polenta
- 1 tsp garlic powder
- Pinch of salt – if desired
- Marinara sauce

FOR THE COATING:
- 250g bread crumbs
- Pinch ground pepper
- ½ tsp garlic powder
- ½ tsp onion powder
- Pinch oregano – dried
- Pinch fresh parsley finely chopped
- Salt and pepper to taste
- 5 ounces mozzarella cheese – this will need to be cut into strips

INSTRUCTIONS

1. Put your water, garlic powder, polenta, and cornflour with the flour in a bowl and mix thoroughly. It should be similar to pancake batter
2. In a separate bowl, mix the breadcrumbs and various herbs, (parsley, oregano, garlic and onion powders, pepper)
3. Cover each of your mozzarella sticks with flour
4. Dip the sticks in the flour mixture and then the breadcrumb mixture. Make sure they are well coated
5. Put them flat on a baking sheet and put them in the freezer for 1 hour
6. Now turn on your air fryer and set it to 200°C
7. Put the mozzarella sticks in the air fryer basket, you may like to line it with parchment paper first. Don't let the sticks touch or stack them
8. Cook for 15 minutes, flipping halfway through
9. Remove and do the second batch

Mac and Cheese Balls

MAKES 24 BALLS
PREP TIME: 15 MINUTES | TOTAL: 3HRS 25 MINUTES
NET CARBS: 9G | PROTEIN: 4G | FIBRE: 1G | FAT: 4G
KCAL: 87

Don't be alarmed, it takes 15 minutes to make and 10 minutes to cook, the rest is refrigerator time

INGREDIENTS

- 750ml water
- 1 bag pasta
- 125ml milk
- 100g butter
- 250g cheddar cheese - grated
- 250g breadcrumbs
- 2 eggs
- Pinch of garlic powder

1. The first step is to cook your pasta. That means putting the water in a pan on the stove and adding the pasta. Let it simmer for 8-10 minutes to ensure the pasta is soft

2. Drain excess water from the pasta and put the pasta back in the pan

3. Keep the mixture on a medium heat as you add the milk, butter, and cheese. Make sure it is all blended

4. Place the pan in the refrigerator to firm the macaroni. It will take approximately 2 hours

5. Preheat your air fryer to 175°C

6. The firm macaroni mix can be easily scooped into balls. Use an ice cream scoop and put them on a lined baking tray

7. Mix the breadcrumbs with the garlic powder to make a coating

8. Beat your eggs and then roll the balls in the eggs followed by the breadcrumb coating

9. Place them in the air fryer basket but line it with parchment paper first. Don't let them touch each other

10. Cook for 12 minutes turning after 8 minutes. They should be golden brown

Greek Fries

SERVES 4
PREP TIME: 10 MINUTES | TOTAL: 50 MINUTES
NET CARBS: 48G | PROTEIN: 11G | FIBRE: 1G | FAT: 14G
KCAL: 350

INGREDIENTS

- 4 medium-sized potatoes
- 200g Greek yoghurt
- ½ cucumber sliced
- 1 tbsp lemon juice
- 100g feta cheese
- 1 tsp minced garlic
- 1 tsp apple cider vinegar
- 2 tsp olive oil
- 1 red onion – sliced
- 12 small tomatoes – these should be halved
- 100g pitted and sliced olives

INSTRUCTIONS

1. Shred the cucumber
2. Mix the yoghurt with lemon juice, garlic, vinegar, and the feta cheese
3. Add the cucumber and set the bowl aside
4. Turn on your air fryer and set it to 200°C
5. Peel the potatoes and chop them into rectangular shapes
6. Put the chopped potatoes in a bowl with the olive oil and shake before transferring them to the air fryer basket
7. Cook for 15 minutes, flipping halfway
8. Drizzle the fries with your yoghurt mix and add olives, tomatoes, and onion to each plate as a garnish

Samosas

SERVES 2-3
PREP TIME: 5 MINUTES | TOTAL: 13 MINUTES
NET CARBS: 28G | PROTEIN: 9G | FIBRE: 2G | FAT: 13G
KCAL: 260

INGREDIENTS

♦ 1 pack of frozen samosas ideally containing 10 samosas
♦ Cooking oil spray

♦ A sauce of your choice
♦ Garnish if desired

INSTRUCTIONS

1. Preheat the air fryer to 180°C
2. Remove the air fryer basket and coat it with the cooking spray to prevent the samosas from sticking
3. Place the samosas in the basket, and make sure they don't touch each other
4. Spray the samosas lightly with the cooking spray
5. Cook for 8 minutes, turning them over after 4 minutes. When you turn them give them another light spray of oil
6. Remove and place on the plate with your chosen sauce and garnish items

Pasta Chips

SERVES 2
PREP TIME: 15 MINUTES | TOTAL: 25 MINUTES
NET CARBS: 23G | PROTEIN: 6G | FIBRE: 1G | FAT: 5G
KCAL: 164

Ever wanted an easy snack that isn't chips? These pasta chips are the perfect solution and fun!

INGREDIENTS

- 250g pasta – ideally farfalle. That's the one that looks like bowties
- 100g melted butter – if you prefer you can use olive oil
- 100g parmesan cheese
- Garlic salt or any other seasoning you enjoy

INSTRUCTIONS

1. Start by boiling some water on the stove. Check your pasta packet for exactly how much water to use
2. Add the pasta and let it simmer for 8 minutes to make it soft
3. Drain the pasta and let it cool for five minutes before transferring it to a bowl
4. Pour the butter or olive oil into the bowl and add the parmesan along with your garlic salt and other seasonings
5. Mix thoroughly to ensure the pasta is fully coated
6. Preheat your air fryer to 200°C
7. Transfer some of the pasta into the air fryer, you don't want more than one layer in the basket at a time
8. Cook for 7-8 minutes, flipping partway through
9. Cook the next batch

Crunchy Fried Pickles

SERVES 3
PREP TIME: 5 MINUTES | TOTAL: 30 MINUTES
NET CARBS: 11G | PROTEIN: 6G | FIBRE: 1G | FAT: 8G
KCAL: 140

INGREDIENTS

- 1 Jar of pickles or two large pickles sliced
- 100g bread crumbs
- 100g parmesan cheese – grated
- 1 tsp ground oregano
- 1 crushed garlic clove
- 1 egg
- 1 tbsp water

INSTRUCTIONS

1. Turn on your air fryer, remove the basket, and set it to 200°C
2. Take your pickle slices and pat them dry with kitchen towel
3. Use a medium-sized bowl and mix your cheese, bread crumbs, ground oregano, and crushed garlic. Make sure it's all properly combined
4. Beat the egg in a glass with the water
5. Take a pickle and dip it in the egg, making sure it is fully coated, then dip it in the bread crumb mixture. Again, make sure it is fully coated
6. Let the pickle sit on the plate while you do the rest
7. Line your air fryer basket with greaseproof paper and put the pickles in, making sure they are not touching each other
8. Cook for 10 minutes and then repeat with the remaining pickles

Salted Crisps

SERVES 4
PREP TIME: 10 MINUTES | TOTAL: 55 MINUTES
NET CARBS: 16G | PROTEIN: 2G | FIBRE: 1G | FAT: 0G
KCAL: 72

INGREDIENTS

- 4 large potatoes – choose anything that's in season or your preferred flavour
- 1 tsp salt
- Cooking oil spray

INSTRUCTIONS

1. Wash your potatoes then peel them
2. Using a potato peeler to take layers off the potatoes, you can make thicker layers for your crisps by using a grater or evenly thinly slicing them with a knife
3. Put the potato slices in a bowl of water and leave them to soak for roughly 15 minutes
4. Replace the water and let them soak for another 15 minutes
5. Turn the air fryer on and set it to 200°C
6. Carefully drain the water from the potatoes and place them on some kitchen towel
7. Dry them with another piece of kitchen towel
8. Sprinkle your salt or any other flavouring you wish
9. Put the potato slices in the air fryer basket but don't put too many in
10. Spray them with just a little oil
11. Cook for 8 minutes and shake before cooking for another 7 minutes
12. Repeat with the remaining potato slices

Steak Jerky

SERVES 4
PREP TIME: 10 MINUTES | TOTAL: 18HRS 25 MINUTES
NET CARBS: 4G | PROTEIN: 21G | FIBRE: 2G | FAT: 5G
KCAL: 147

INGREDIENTS

- 500g of beef sirloin steak – you're going to cut it into thin strips so you can use pre-shredded steak
- 100ml soy sauce
- 50g brown sugar
- 1 tbsp seasoning, preferably steak seasoning
- 1 tsp Worcestershire sauce
- Salt and pepper if desired

INSTRUCTIONS

1. After cutting the steak into small strips put it in a pan with the soy sauce, brown sugar, Worcestershire sauce, and your seasoning
2. Add a small amount of water and seal the bag
3. Shake to ensure the steak strips are coated in the ingredients and then leave to marinate. It's best to put it in the fridge as you'll want to marinate it for 8 hours
4. Take your air fryer basket and find skewers that will fit across it, resting on the holes on either side. Make sure they are also short enough to fit inside the fryer
5. Turn on your air fryer and let it get to 95°C
6. Remove the beef strips from the bag and thread them onto the skewers, you'll get several on each strip but leave a space between them
7. Thread the skewers into the air fryer basket ensuring they are resting safely on each side
8. Lower the basket into the heated air fryer and cook for 2 hours
9. It's a good idea to move the skewers around every 30 minutes
10. After two hours lower the air fryer temperature to 90°C and cook the strips for an additional 15 minutes
11. Let them cool for five minutes then enjoy

Italian Ratatouille

SERVES 4
PREP TIME: 25 MINUTES | TOTAL: 55 MINUTES
NET CARBS: 10G | PROTEIN: 2G | FIBRE: 1G | FAT: 4G
KCAL: 79

INGREDIENTS

- 1 small aubergine – chopped into small pieces
- 1 butternut squash – you'll need to cut this into small pieces
- 2 tomatoes – also chopped into small pieces
- 2 peppers – ideally different colours and also cut into small pieces
- 1 onion – unsurprisingly chopped into small pieces
- 1 tbsp dried oregano
- 1 crushed clove of garlic
- 1 tbsp olive oil
- A few drops of vinegar
- Salt and pepper to taste

INSTRUCTIONS

1. Plug in your air fryer and set it to 200°C
2. Grab a bowl and put the chopped pieces of aubergine in it with the butternut squash, peppers, onion, and tomatoes
3. Mix it all thoroughly
4. Sprinkle the olive oil, vinegar, oregano, garlic, and any salt and pepper you desire into the bowl
5. Mix again
6. Put the mixture into a baking dish that fits inside the basket of your air fryer
7. Lower the basket into your machine and cook for 16 minutes, stirring halfway through
8. Cook for another five minutes and check to see if they are tender, if not cook for another 5 minutes and so on
9. It's advisable to let the ratatouille rest for several minutes before you serve it as a delicious snack

Flavoured Potato Wedges

SERVES 4
PREP TIME: 10 MINUTES | TOTAL: 30 MINUTES
NET CARBS: 19G | PROTEIN: 2G | FIBRE: 2G | FAT: 4G
KCAL: 115

INGREDIENTS

- 2 large potatoes – you can choose your preferred variety
- 1 tbsp olive oil
- Pinch of salt and pepper if desired
- Your choice of herbs or seasoning

INSTRUCTIONS

1. Start with your potatoes, you'll want to wash them and pat them dry
2. Make sure they are fully dried before cutting them into wedges, you should get 12 from each potato, if you don't, use extra potatoes. It's okay to leave the skin on
3. Turn on the air fryer and set the temperature to 200°C
4. Put your cut potatoes in a bowl and drizzle with the olive oil
5. Add your choice of herbs or spices. Some great options are rosemary, paprika, or even curry powder
6. Mix the wedges gently to ensure you don't break them but they are fully coated
7. Place the wedges in the air fryer, they need to be flat in the bottom and not touching, you'll probably need to do them in batches
8. Drop the basket into the air fryer, close the lid and cook for 20 minutes, flipping them over halfway through, they should be golden
9. Let them cool slightly before enjoying

Potato Tots

SERVES 24
PREP TIME: 15 MINUTES | TOTAL: 60 MINUTES
NET CARBS: 5G | PROTEIN: 0G | FIBRE: 0G | FAT: 2G
KCAL: 21

INGREDIENTS

- ◆ 2 large sweet potatoes – you'll need to peel them first
- ◆ 1 tsp Cajun spice seasoning or your preferred seasoning
- ◆ Salt and pepper as desired
- ◆ Cooking oil spray

INSTRUCTIONS

1. Start by bringing a pan of water to the boil over your stove
2. Once it's boiling out your sweet potatoes in the water and boil for 15 minutes, they should still be firm but soft enough to put a fork in
3. Drain the water from the pan and let the potatoes cool
4. Turn on your air fryer and set it to 200°C
5. Once the potatoes are cooled, you'll want to grate them, use a large grater setting
6. Make sure all the grated pieces are in a bowl and add your seasoning and any salt and pepper you desire
7. Line your air fryer basket with greaseproof paper
8. Take a bit of the mixture in your hand and form a small cube with it. Once done add it to the basket
9. Fill the basket, with just one layer and make sure the tots aren't touching each other
10. Put them in the air fryer and cook for 8 minutes; remove them and let them cool as you do the next batch
11. Enjoy by themselves or with any sauce you desire

Butternut Fries

SERVES 6
PREP TIME: 15 MINUTES | TOTAL: 30 MINUTES
NET CARBS: 29G | PROTEIN: 3G | FIBRE: 1G | FAT: 5G
KCAL: 150

INGREDIENTS

- 2 medium butternut squashes
- 2 tbsp olive oil
- 2 crushed cloves of garlic
- 1 tbsp paprika
- Salt and pepper to taste

INSTRUCTIONS

1. Start by washing the sweet potatoes and patting them dry with kitchen towel
2. Then, cut them into slices, the size of regular fries. You can leave the skin on or remove it, depending on your preference
3. Plug in and turn on the air fryer, it needs to be 200°C
4. Find a large bowl and put your butternut squash in it
5. Add your oil, paprika, garlic, and any salt and pepper you wish
6. Toss all the ingredients together to ensure the sweet potato pieces are coated in the mixture
7. Line your air fryer basket with greaseproof paper
8. Arrange the butternut fries in the basket and cook for 20 minutes, you'll need to shake them every 5 minutes to ensure they cook evenly
9. Lift the basket out when the fries are golden and serve straight away

Lobster Tails

SERVES 2
PREP TIME: 5 MINUTES | TOTAL: 15 MINUTES
NET CARBS: 18G | PROTEIN: 8G | FIBRE: 1G | FAT: 12G
KCAL: 109

INGREDIENTS

- 2 lobster tails – any size
- 50g butter, preferably unsalted
- 1 clove garlic crushed
- 1 tsp lemon juice
- Small amount of freshly chopped chives
- Salt and pepper if desired

INSTRUCTIONS

1. Start by turning on your air fryer, it needs to be set to 180°C
2. Now put the butter in a bowl with the garlic, chives, lemon juice, and any salt or pepper you wish
3. Take each lobster tail and remove the shell, it's best to do this by cutting it off, bashing it can leave pieces in the meat
4. Spread the butter mix across both sides of each lobster tail
5. Put a piece of greaseproof paper in the bottom of your air fryer basket and then add the lobster tails, make sure they are not touching each other
6. Lower the basket into the air fryer and cook for 8 minutes
7. Turn the tails over halfway through the cooking process and add more butter if you wish
8. They are ready to eat straight away as a snack or part of a main meal

Disclaimer

This book contains opinions and ideas of the author and is meant to teach the reader informative and helpful knowledge while due care should be taken by the user in the application of the information provided. The instructions and strategies are possibly not right for every reader and there is no guarantee that they work for everyone. Using this book and implementing the information/recipes therein contained is explicitly your own responsibility and risk. This work with all its contents, does not guarantee correctness, completion, quality or correctness of the provided information. Misinformation or misprints cannot be completely eliminated.

EXCLUSIVE BONUS

40 Weight Loss Recipes

&

14 Days Meal Plan

Scan the QR-Code and receive
the FREE download:

Printed in Great Britain
by Amazon

16480871R00082